Bethlehem Lu...
Two Harbors, Minn.

WHO'S RUNNING YOUR LIFE?

WHO'S RUNNING YOUR LIFE?

Marge & Erling Wold

AUGSBURG PUBLISHING HOUSE
MINNEAPOLIS, MINNESOTA

WHO'S RUNNING YOUR LIFE?

Copyright © 1976 Augsburg Publishing House

Library of Congress Catalog Card No. 78-3863

International Standard Book No. 0-8066-1540-0

All rights reserved. No part of this book may be used or reproduced in any manner whatsoever without written permission except in the case of brief quotations embodied in critical articles and reviews. For information address Augsburg Publishing House, 426 South Fifth Street, Minneapolis, Minnesota 55415.

Scripture quotations unless otherwise noted are from the Revised Standard Version of the Bible, copyright 1946, 1952, and 1971 by the Division of Christian Education of the National Council of Churches.

MANUFACTURED IN THE UNITED STATES OF AMERICA

Contents

Introduction 7

1. Where Are You Now? 11

2. How Did I Get Here? 23

3. How Do You Feel? 37

4. What Choice Do I Have? 53

5. What's God's Will for Me? 67

6. What Makes Dreams Come True? 83

7. How Are Big Decisions Made? 103

8. How Do I Get It All Together and Keep Going? 117

Bethlehem Lutheran Church
Two Harbors, Minn.

Introduction

"Really, Erling, who's running our life?"
Erling was lying on the couch, stretched out in utter exhaustion at the end of the day. It was Monday, normally a pastor's day off, but since our assistant had left two weeks before to accept another assignment, Erling's responsibilities in the parish had doubled.

The Friday before, we had returned to California after a series of speaking engagements in the Minneapolis area. A capacity crowd had filled a suburban high school auditorium when we spoke on Tuesday evening of that week. We had each appeared twice before on that same day to smaller groups.

On Wednesday we both spoke four times to four hundred women at a conference in Stillwater, Minnesota. Then on Friday, we left Minneapolis to return to California—but on different planes! Erling took off for Los Angeles to prepare for the weekend church activities an hour before my plane left for San Francisco, where I had two more speaking engagements, one in the Napa Valley and the other in the city itself. I came home on Monday to face a manuscript deadline the next Thursday, and the following weekend we were both due to speak at another convention in the San Fernando Valley!

Now it was the end of that Monday on which I had come home. Erling's legs twitched as they sometimes do now when he's very tired. Ever since his neck was broken he's had trouble with his leg muscles at the end of a strenuous day. *Just two-and-a-half years since that time of total paralysis for him and I feel like we've lived a lifetime in its shadow,* I thought.

"Really, Erling, who *is* running our lives?"

The echo of the question I'd asked hung in the air between us. Neither one of us was willing to tackle the answer and be forced to deal with all of the complexities it suggested. Were we living with the reality of Erling's accident and its effects on his physical and emotional energies? Here we were, harder at work than ever, as though that event had never taken place, as though nothing had changed in our lives, as though we had not learned any lessons from it. Somehow the current of life had pulled us back into itself before we had taken time to plant our feet firmly in the middle of its stream and ask ourselves that question, "Who's running my life?"

Unless we force ourselves to stop periodically and do this, we are likely to drift with the whims and caprices of life, dashed haphazardly against the boulders over which it flows, often ending up broken and exhausted in its shallows.

Such seemed the case at this point in our lives. Somewhere there had to be an answer which said, "With the help of God, *we* are in charge of running our lives!"

Undeniably, a death and resurrection experience does force one to examine actions and motives with greater honesty. Having faced the piercing light of eternity, we recall previous attitudes and behaviors and conclude: "Phony! Beware of misrepresentation!" Choices we had made unthinkingly in the past now need evaluation in terms of our changed circumstances and new purposes. The reason given so easily to explain our former decisions—"because it's God's will"—is now carefully tested before it's casually used.

Were we following such an exhausting schedule to deny that the broken neck had really affected Erling's ability to perform as he had before the accident? Were we "choosing" to accept every invitation that came to share our crisis experience because *others* needed to hear of God's miracle-working grace—or because *we* needed to speak? Were we back on the old "rat race" because we felt compelled to witness to our conviction that God does mark each sparrow that falls—or because we hadn't learned mature ways of saying no? Were we being propelled by God's Spirit into wholehearted spiritual service—or were we compulsive "workaholics" enjoying the rewards of exhausted martyrdom?

This book chronicles our struggle to answer the questions of our purposes, choices, and motives and to touch base again with our own wills and their operation in the context of God's will. Because we have talked to so many others who are asking the same questions and because many have been willing to share their own learnings with us, we are convinced that what we write will help you create your own unique answer to our question, "Who's running your life?"

And perhaps there may even be some of you who read just because you were intrigued by the title question. You may never have thought that God had anything at all to do with the running of your life, but now in reading this book, you may discover that he's been there all along, guiding its circumstances and the choices you've made!

1.

Where Are You Now?

MARGE: *Where are you now?* I heard the words in my mind as clearly as my eyes were seeing the sharp, rain-washed outlines of the tropical foliage through which I walked. In my preoccupation with other more immediate concerns, I brushed the question aside impatiently.

Anxiety quickened my climb up the mountain path to Chiang Kai-shek's simple chapel overlooking Sun-Moon Lake. The time was two months after we had started our serious pondering of the question, "Who's running our lives?" I was due this morning to give a third in a series of Bible studies to Chinese university students who had come together from all over Taiwan for this retreat. A heavy schedule of listening to their personal stories the day before had kept me from feeling adequately prepared for this morning. Sharpening the edge of my anxiety was the fact that the friend who had faithfully awakened me every other day (I had forgotten to bring an alarm clock) had this morning forgotten about me. So I had scrambled to get ready, awakening just in time to hear the people in the room next to mine hurrying to make the last call for breakfast.

Already the summer sun was warming the humid air, and beads of sweat dampened my face and neck. The thin mountain air ached its way into my hungry lungs and dizzied my brain.

What a strange question to come into my mind now, just when I need to be concentrating on what I'm going to say in a few minutes, I thought. *I must really be needing more oxygen!*

But the question clung leech-like to my consciousness. *Where are you now?*

So insistently did it demand a reply that I stopped in my panting flight, aware of one of those scalp-prickling moments of illumination that can only be compared to finding a puzzle piece and recognizing that it's the key to a whole section of puzzle that had been closed before.

"Why, of course! I'm *here*—here in Taiwan, in the Republic of China, about to give a Bible study to Chinese young people!" And with that recognition I knew what I was going to talk about that morning.

I can almost hear you saying, "What's so profound about knowing where you were that morning? What's the big revelation? I thought we were going to get a prophetic insight of earth-shaking importance!"

That moment of illumination which came to me on the snail-infested mountain path in the middle of Taiwan brought a new perspective to the question we'd been asking, "Who's running my life?"

To help you understand that perspective I need to take you back many years to my graduation from college. Young women like me who sensed God's call to preach and teach the Word in those days had few options in the church. The most viable one was a "letter of call" from some "foreign" mission board to carry on Christian work in another land.

I felt fortunate, on graduation, to receive such a letter to go to China as a Bible teacher, but a world war was being waged in the Pacific, and no single young women were being given passports to that part of the world unless they were nurses.

My disappointment was keen. I was young and—I thought—capable and well qualified to make a significant impact on the spiritual life of China! I went into nurses' training; I traveled as a speaker to youth groups encouraging young people to volunteer for overseas service; I got married and had a family. I knew, as my life moved on, that I would never get to China as a missionary.

But my interest in and love for the Chinese people continued and I became closely involved with the work of Pastor Calvin Chao who had been forced to flee the Chinese mainland with his family during the communist revolution and eventually came to the Los Angeles area to begin work with Chinese university students in this country, many of them also refugees. With these friends I had helped edit a bilingual magazine which was circulated wherever Chinese students were free to read Christian literature in this country and the Far East.

Then early in 1975 came the invitation to give Bible studies to university students in Taiwan. Because of other pressures I almost didn't go. Never once did I make any connection beforehand between that invitation and my long-forgotten, yellow-with-age letter of call!

On the mountain path in Taiwan the third morning of the retreat the connection was made for me. The insistent question thrust into my consciousness by God's Spirit forced me to check the course my life had taken and once again to see my life's meaning and purpose from a "larger than life" perspective. Another loose end had been tied up, and a conviction that God had remembered and given me the "desires of my heart" (Ps. 37:4-5), even when I had committed those desires to the dusty dreams of the past, filled me with awe.

Where are *you* now?

God puts us into history at a very special time for each one of us and for a very special purpose. We have in our selves a sense of our own identity and of our own personality. *You* know that you're not Marge Wold or Erling Wold, and *we* know that we're not you. Each one of us was born with a consciousness of our own identity.

Have you ever wondered, as we have, "Why wasn't I born 4000 years ago or 400 years ago or 400 years in the future—if there is to be a future then? Why am I here today at this particular time in history?"

We each know the date of our birth, but as yet none of us knows what that last date on our obituary is going to be. Nor do we have any choice in either date—unless we take our own lives. The only part of our epitaph that we have anything to say about is that dash in between. The dates at either end may prove to be the same for some of us, but never will that line in between be the same. *Your* lifeline is as different from ours as our fingerprints or our voiceprints. For none of us will that line between the dates of our birth and our death carry out that definition we learned in geometry: "A straight line is the shortest distance between two distinct points."

Some day those two distinct points will be neatly tacked down for us, but our lifelines will not be neat lines in between if we draw them on paper the way they are lived. Unexpected jogs and detours defy even a two-dimensional line, and our lifeline drawing may have to leap right off the paper to a point somewhere out in space.

Some lifelines are unbelievably short. Just the matter of a few hours, a few years. Walk through your local graveyard and ponder the dates inscribed on the markers there. Some lifelines are very long, and when people live a long time they may have to face the question, "Why am I still alive when everyone else I ever knew, including my whole family, has died?"

ERLING: At the time I broke my neck, the president of our national church body, a brilliant man in his forties, whose keen mind and world-encompassing concerns had made him the center of many Christian dreams, was taken ill with a rare disease. Many prayers were said for both of us. We loved the same Lord, and both of us had dedicated our lives to the service of our church. *I* recovered almost completely from my total paralysis; *he* died. His death aroused some deep questionings in me. Why had I lived while he who served in a seemingly much more strategic position had died?

The enigma of God's dealings with his creation still mystifies me. I can easily theologize that questioning by quoting the words of Isaiah that God's ways are not our ways and God's thoughts are not our thoughts. But underneath all the intellectual assent, I still ponder the mystery and hang on in the middle of questions and pain only because of my conviction, "He knows what is best for me! Lord, help me to believe that." I go on knowing that it's only where I am *now* that's relevant. I *am* living; I *am* here for a purpose, even though I'm not always aware at the moment of the uniqueness of that purpose for me. But daily the conviction that that purpose exists drives me on to search it out and live it.

So strange, those inexplicable twists and turns of every individual life. Tragedies and joys, ups and downs, all these come and go. The plotting of one's lifeline may result in a smooth and even tracing or in an erratically irregular graph. The faintly delicate tracery of one life may seem eclipsed by another's adventure-packed heaviness. The lifeline that is barely two-dimensional in form may pass unnoticed up against one that flips out in four or five dimensions.

"Where am I?" That's usually the first question asked by a patient coming awake after having been anesthetized. Whenever anyone has been unconscious for any length of time, that question marks the first awareness of reality as evidence of returning consciousness. Have you ever experienced that sense of disorientation that comes when you waken from a sound sleep in a strange bedroom and don't remember where you are? The window is in the wrong place and the door is not where it should be! To never ask the question, "Where am I?" is to remain unconscious of the ongoing realities of one's own existence and of life around one.

MARGE: For me it was a profound revelation that morning in Taiwan to realize that the God into whose hands I had committed my lifeline when I was 18 years old was able to faithfully keep the promise that I was to go to China as a Bible teacher. Isn't it amazing that the only time in my life that I have been invited to a foreign land to give Bible studies the invitation came from the Republic of China? Why not Ethiopia? Why had some country in Europe not claimed my "talents"?

The lesson I learned from that Taiwan experience is that time is measured in each lifeline from two perspectives—God's and mine. After all, God operates from the timelessness of eternity (we could say that God has "all the time in the world"), but I have only linear time to deal with as I live it out in that lifeline between the dates of my birth and death.

That day in Taiwan convinced me that God had postponed my going to China because he knew the right time for me to go. The group I had originally been scheduled to travel with to China when I finished college was interned in a Japanese prison camp in the Philippines for three years. Some of them never got to China, and some went to other places.

My goal wasn't realized when I thought it should have been, but looking back I know that at the time I finished college I was in no way mature enough to have lived alone in some remote village. I was too tied to family, too dependent on others for emotional support. I doubt if I would have survived!

Looking ahead we can't always see the course our lives have taken. Checking the wake of a ship gives more of a sense of direction than looking down at the splashing waters as they're cut by the prow.

Could it be that the kind of Bible message I am now capable of bringing was best saved to be heard by some young person not yet born in the 1940s and whose place in history will be affected by what I said that morning in the Republic of China? I dare to believe that.

Christian lives are best lived without too much concern for careful "plotting" of the lifeline. God's Spirit invests them with a quality of serendipity when we are ready at any moment to lose our lives for the sake of Jesus (Luke 9:24).

We sometimes identify this as a "throwaway" life. Think about the people whom the world remembers.

Aren't they likely to be the ones to whom others have at one time said, "Think of all you could be—and also all the money you could make!—if only you weren't throwing your life away on that crazy cause!"

Can't you hear his friends and family saying that to Albert Schweitzer when he decided to "throw away his life" on a lot of "ignorant natives" in the steamy African jungles? Yet today very few remember that Schweitzer was an undisputed authority on the life and works of the philosopher Goethe and a great Bach organist, but millions remember that he built a hospital in Lambarene, and some are even moved to make pilgrimages to that monument to God's love for *all* people as it worked through one man's life.

Some of you have already had people say that to you. Perhaps you've begun to see your life in a new perspective: you've been gripped by a vision of how your talents and abilities can be used in some wildly wonderful way for God and humankind—and what happens? The "cold water" treatment cools your dreams with the words, "What do you want to throw your life away on something like that for?"

The most throwaway life ever lived was the life of Jesus. In his desire to live every minute for God and people, he never considered his own safety first. How many times did he tell his hearers, "Don't be so careful about your life!" He meant it just that way: "Don't be so care-full—full of care, full of anxiety, full of fear, full of anxiousness about your life. Throw your life away; be willing to lose it for my sake and the Good News you've been given to share for the life of the world! Let go of your life because if you try to save it, you'll lose it in ultimate ways."

The super-religious Pharisees who heard him make

statements like this were so terribly care-full that they hedged their lives around with hundreds of laws to be sure they wouldn't make any mistakes. The laws became fences preventing any contact with "unclean" foods and "unclean" people. The Pharisees made sure that they were never guilty of any actions that might jeopardize their Saran-wrapped lives.

Our country is full of beautiful church structures which were once a gathering place for hundreds of worshippers. Now perhaps 50 people come together on Sunday mornings with the basic purpose of protecting the life of the church by resisting change. Like the Pharisees they fence themselves about with traditions and rules until death consumes them and the congregation. The secret of life in the church, as in individuals, lies in giving itself away in reckless abandon for the life of the world. Pride in "our own kind of people" must lose itself in love for "them"—all of us "sinners."

The Los Angeles newspapers carried a feature story about a man who, after experiencing several burglaries, had sold out his business, took his money out of the bank, and moved to the desert some 200 miles away from the city. With 50 miles between himself and every other human, without paved roads leading anywhere nearby, he lives alone in the little fortress he built, carefully guarding his life and his possessions with a variety of firearms and ammunition. He's being very care-full with his life!

Jesus never advocated a "do-away" life. You don't live the throw-away life by doing away with it—deliberately taking an overdose of drugs or using a gun to blow out your brains. Not that. In fact, that kind of action might be the ultimate carefulness because it announces, "I've protected my life by doing away with it! Nothing can touch me now." Being afraid to live is the most common reason for protecting one's life, and you can protect your life by doing away with it.

That kind of action has nothing in common with the throw-away life, although the latter might lead to an untimely death. After all, Jesus was only 33 years old when he was crucified for not being more careful with his life. Joan of Arc, in her fearless honesty about her godly visions, refused to be careful of her young life and was burned to death by the religious leaders of her day. If the papal edict against Luther had been implemented, he, too, would have died as a young man.

Where are you now? Jesus reminds us to live for today without taking thought for tomorrow and without looking back along the furrow we've plowed. The past and the future exist only in our fantasies.

MARGE: Even as I write about that morning in Taiwan, I realize that it already exists only in my fantasies. That mountain path event is already dimming in its nerve-tingling illumination of the moment. Other events have come between it and the present, each one casting its own illumination on my lifeline.

I think sometimes of the frustration that could have dominated my life if I had lived with regret for having "missed my calling" by not getting to China when I thought I should have gone. How often I meet folks in my travels who sigh about the opportunities they missed. They often say, "I'm a frustrated writer myself (or painter or concert pianist or speaker.)" Even though their present life may be filled with all manner of good things, they permit the *one* thing they didn't get in the past to destroy their happiness in the present.

In Taipei, I saw the tiny house in which missionary

Clara Jones had lived when she was forced to leave her work on the Chinese mainland. She didn't just sit there and sigh about the lost past and the work she had left behind. Her little home was across the street from the largest university in Taiwan, and she began working with and ministering to the students there. As a result her little house is now almost hidden behind a two-story student center, by a large church building and parish hall, by a several-story-high men's dormitory and a matching women's dormitory.

It's fun to look at old slide pictures and home movies and photo albums every once in a while, especially if they lead us to say, "We've sure come a long way since that time, haven't we?" and then to close the book, put the pictures away, and be able to add, "But today is God's day for me, complete with its own pain, its own joys and its own expectations. I don't want to go back."

For each of us the possibilities for having this kind of conviction about our own lifelines exists. A dramatic life? A quiet life? Each life has meaning all its own. Whatever the shape of your lifeline, it is uniquely yours. You are living it and making your own mark in time. Where, then, are you now?

REFLECTION EXERCISE

1. Draw your own lifeline.

Where were the "up" moments, the "down" ones? Where was the grace of God especially real to you? Close your eyes and recall the feelings of those grace-filled moments.

What is your first memory?

Where is the line heavy with meaning; where is it light and faint in your memory?

Mark the places where you felt you were in charge of your own life. Where did you feel that God and you were working closely in the running of your life? Where did you feel that forces beyond your control were in charge? When were you surprised by the Spirit's "serendipity"?

2. Where is "now" for you? Who's in charge of your "now"?

3. How would you classify your life? Do you feel that you underestimate the unique significance of your own life and feel that others have made a more significant mark in history? Whose judgment matters? Do your feelings about your life have anything to do with now, or are they due to your reflections and fantasies about missed opportunities in your past?

4. Can you get in touch with your feelings now?

5. What experiences have you had which make you say, "Aha, I see now where God has been working in my life all the while!"

6. Is one of those times right now?

2.

How Did I Get Here?

The circumstances of our birth and early life are unchangeable. Nothing we do later changes these facts. Of course, we can deny our past, lie about it, change our names, and pretend that wasn't "me." We can scream, weep, and joke about it; we can forgive and accept it, but we can never change it. The sunshine and shadow of the past affect the climate of our present.

Do we then resign ourselves to our "fate"? Does the configuration of stars under which I was born forever control my destiny? As surely as the "untouchables" of India were at one time locked into their demeaning caste, so we can lock ourselves into despair or pride because of the circumstances of our birth and early life. For too many of us—yes, even Christians—the feeling that all is "fated" from birth to death immobilizes our will to choose.

We point to Judas. Doesn't the Apostle Peter say that Judas betrayed Jesus and then hanged himself because "the Scripture had to be fulfilled, which the Holy Spirit spoke beforehand by the mouth of David" (Acts 1:16)? What chance did Judas have if he was "fated" to betray the Lord and be damned?

Churches have split on the question of "fate," only Christians call it "foreordination." Always the Christian must remember that God's primary concern is that *all* should be saved and come to the knowledge of the truth (1 Tim. 2:4). The fact that God knows beforehand what course our lives will take does not nullify the conscious choices we make once we know that we have the power to choose our ways.

At any time Judas could have repented. Jesus gave him opportunities up to the final betrayal scene with his question, "Judas, would you betray the Son of man with a kiss?" (Luke 22:48).

The despair of resignation cannot dominate our lives if we recognize that in each one of us is a unique "me" that is totally different from every other being on the face of the earth now, different from any other person who has ever lived and therefore destined to make a unique pilgrimage.

Occasionally we benefit by making a journey back into our beginnings to claim again the experiences of those early years as a way of understanding the "me" that lives and feels and makes choices in the present. Those early experiences are neither right nor wrong. They just *are*. It's meaningless for people to come to us and say, "This is what you *should have* experienced." We experienced what we experienced. Whatever we experienced comes out of the context of our own lives and differs for each of us. All we can do is to help each other get in touch with the reality of those unchangeable experiences of our pasts without judging, without blaming, without belittling or magnifying them, but simply to help us understand some of the reasons we act as we do in the present.

MARGE: I was seven years old when I first realized that I was "me." I don't really know why it happened at that time, but I can see the setting so clearly. We were living in a small town named Hartford about 125 miles around the southern tip of Lake Michigan from Chicago. Pa had decided that the city was no place for him to bring up his growing family, so he sold his little trucking business and bought an acreage in Michigan.

Mental pictures click into focus: an apple and cherry orchard, a vineyard of Concord grapes, and a large open area which we called a "campground." Besides the small one-and-a-half-storey house, there was a "refreshment stand" where tourists could buy soft drinks, candy, ice cream, and Crackerjacks; a small two-pump Sinclair gas station; and three "cottages" for travelers who needed a place to spend the night. Model T Fords and Oldsmobile "touring cars" with isinglass snap-on side curtains whizzed by at speeds up to 30 m.p.h. on U.S. Highway 12 which ran within 25 feet of our house. Every night, exactly at 9:30, a distant train whistle announced the imminent arrival of the *Kalamazoo Flyer,* a string of lighted coach windows moving along an unseen track a mile to the south. Life in that town could not fail to be as safely predictable as that train whistle, my parents thought.

Even now when I want to focus on a particularly happy event in my life, I'm likely to pull out of my memory file a picture from the early days of those Michigan years: walking to school waist deep in snow-filled ditches; getting a bottle of cold Nehi pop from ma on a hot summer day; sliding down the fire escape from the second floor of the red brick school on the other side of town (the fire escapes were metal chutes, ancient forerunners of the plastic inflatable chutes now used for emergency evacuation of airplane passengers).

In this setting my first moment of self-recognition came—the moment in which I saw my own uniqueness and recognized that my journey in the pilgrimage of life would be distinctively different from that of any other human being around me, even from my own brothers and sisters.

It happened one day when I was home from school with a childhood illness. To keep from having to run upstairs to care for me, Ma had made a bed on the couch in the downstairs parlor. With the sun flooding the plush, overstuffed room through the starched stretcher-stiff lace curtains, that sense of my own special destiny flooded me.

"How," I asked my seven-year-old self, "did I come to be born to this particular family? How did ma and pa get to be *my* mother and father and not some other ma and pa? Why did I have one older brother, and what happened to that older brother and sister about whose death we had been told so often?"

So mysterious, all of it, and so irrevocably, unchangeably set forever. I would never be anyone else, born in any other family. This *me* was the me that would always be. What was the mystery that had placed my identity in this particular body? How was it that I looked out at the world through the eyes in this body? The things that I saw, were they seen also by others? Did I see things differently or the same as everyone else?

What brought that moment of startling awareness to me? Perhaps it was the result of the flat-out statements made by my Catholic relatives (my father was a devout Roman Catholic during my childhood) that, *at age seven,* one became "accountable" for one's sins. I remember approaching that seventh birthday with a great deal of hesitation and not a little fear! What would I feel like when I was accountable for my sins? Indeed, what were *sins?* A sad sense of aloneness swept over me whenever I thought of that day that was to separate me in some mysterious way from my parents who, up to this point in time, had presumably been responsible for my sins.

On that day in the sunny parlor, a scary feeling urged me to pull back from that unknown territory in which I was seeing myself so clearly. At the same time I had to fight the temptation to lose myself in the mysteries of my own inner consciousness—and in that awesome Being who had made me to be *me,* and to whom I was now responsible.

But reality returned with the sound of ma pumping water in the kitchen and firing up the wood stove for dinner. Those safe, comforting sounds tempered the excitement of my new self-knowledge, and I napped, glad that I was who I was in that home.

Many decades were to pass before I was to hear the term "identity crisis" and realize that this was the moment in which my identity became real to me, my first conscious step on my own unique earth-journey with my Creator.

ERLING: The white-flecked skies of the Dakotas stretched over my childhood world. I enjoyed the wind and wonder of that world where the summer grain preened and ruffled itself in vast golden expanses as far as my child-high eyes could see. Yet in some ways that world narrowed when winter came—bitter cold, inhibiting, compressive.

In that wintry confinement, I sometimes moved off into fantasy. Reading always intrigued me, but a small town with a tiny library provided haphazard opportunities for indulging that appetite. I discovered another book-loving friend in the only physician in our town, a Canadian who had lost his hearing. He was a caring person with an immense love for the people of that community, but his handicap kept him attached to his office and the nurse-secretary who relayed messages to him. In the time between house calls he read endless Western and detective stories, passing his pulp-magazine world on to me.

In the fantasies this world evoked, I could see myself identified in so many roles. I was a cowboy riding up on horseback to the door of my church (which was right there next door to my house), the adored center of attraction at the Sunday service. I envisioned myself walking down the aisles in my cowboy regalia, a Very Important Person (a champion of justice, naturally!) in the eyes of all who saw me.

Or again, I was Lester Lieth, hero of those pulp-magazine detective stories. Lester, an immensely rich man, was aware that his butler was in reality an incognito police officer. The butler always read aloud to Lester the news in the daily press. The master detective's mind would focus perceptively on some incident from the news, especially those items describing how someone had been robbed by a criminal. Lester Lieth (of course!) always successfully apprehended the criminal and returned the stolen loot to the rightful owner. The police, informed by the butler, were inevitably foiled in their efforts to solve the crimes before Lester did.

Lester was my paper hero—the perennial Good Samaritan, doing his good deed in his own way.

MARGE: Chicago was really our home, and we moved back there right in the middle of the Great Depression, a sadder and wiser family. The high hopes which had driven my parents out of Chicago to the rural paradise of Michigan's orchard country had been shattered. Lost was the lovely apple orchard in which I could climb a tree and nestle to read in the rough arm of a fruit-heavy branch. The thick gooseberry patch and the grapevines which made such fantastic spidery places to play Hide-Go-Seek—all this was gone, lost in the financial chaos of the Thirties. Even more devastating was the loss of a two-and-a-half-year-old brother who had been my special little shadow.

When we came back to Chicago, he was dead.

Bright's disease, a deadly kidney malady in those pre-antibiotic days, sent Gilbert and ma to a Chicago hospital. For three months they fought their lonely battles with uremic poisoning. Ma won hers; Gilbert lost his.

Of all my childhood summers, that summer alone can I recall with any clarity. Our family was separated for the first time, except for those overnight visits to various aunts when the "stork" was due to make a drop at our house. Pa sent us children away to live with relatives so that he could be free to stay with his dying son and wife.

I was taken with my older brother Frank and young sister Esther to live with the family of my father's cousin, a tall angular woman we called Aunt Clara. Her husband, Uncle Rich, at one time a brakeman in the Cicero switchyards, had some years before fallen under a train and had his leg cut off. One of the whispered legends about him related how he had taken his own belt off and tied it around the stump to stop himself from bleeding to death before help could arrive. A tremendously tough and stern man (or so we children perceived him), he frightened us out of our wits. A tyrant goaded by pain, he yelled orders loudly at his two daughters and us.

The loneliness of the attic room in which the girls were put haunted me for years afterwards. Whenever summer storms swept across the Chicago area, I would hear again the mournful drumming of rain on that attic roof and see once more the tormented shadows of wind-tossed trees dancing in agony to the sobs we muffled under the blankets.

That summer was to introduce me to my own mortality. Somehow my sorrow over Gilbert's untimely death forced me, for the next half-dozen years, to wrestle with questions that whispered under all conscious thought: "What's it all about? Why live? Why be born and grow up and get sick and die?"

Gilbert's body lay in its little coffin in a corner of the living room in my grandmother's Chicago flat. Unnoticed by the preoccupied adults, I sat for hours in a corner of that living room, not really comprehending the fact that Gilbert—small, blond, lovable—would never again get up out of that motionless sleep and come running to me with childish demands on my time. Guilt darkened my thoughts with memories of the times I had hidden so he wouldn't bother me with requests to read stories or play with him.

Death appeared grim and unrelenting in its stranglehold on life. The mirrors in the house were covered with sheets lest, as my superstitious Grandmother Pedersen said, "the image of the dead should stay on them," but nothing was available to keep that coffin from printing its image on my heart. The smell of a certain kind of rose still reminds me of grandma's living room and the small coffin in the corner.

We never went back to Michigan. Ma could not face that place again. Besides, in those pre-hospital insurance days, the cost of illness had eaten up savings, and mortgage payments could not be made. So we moved back to Chicago, and pa got a job as a truck driver and worked hard to keep his large family provided with life's necessities. His own father had died when he was a boy of eleven so pa was used to hard work.

I can identify so wholeheartedly with the fact that the teen years are far from being the happiest years of our lives, and the city of Chicago was to be forever associated in my mind with death, despair, and meaninglessness.

Meaninglessness. Not that we didn't have fun even in hard times, but my own uncertainty about the meaning of life spoiled even laughter and achievement. A post-high-school job in a downtown bank only deepened my despair. The long hour-and-a-half ride to and from work every morning and evening became a lesson in mass depression to my 17-year-old sensitivities.

Poverty and unremittingly hard work branded the seamed faces and slumped bodies on crowded streetcars and elevated trains. No one talked. The silence, broken only by screeching metal wheels, clanging trolley bells, and the bellowing conductor, was heavy with despair.

"God, if you're around, get me out of this!" I cried one desperate night when suicide seemed the only alternative to a meaningless life.

God *was* around. My cry was answered within a week with a miraculous offer of a job at a Lutheran college in northeastern Iowa and the opportunity for an education that had been a total impossibility before became the door to meaning. At Luther College Jesus came alive in my life, and he destroyed meaninglessness for me forever just as surely as he had destroyed death by his resurrection!

I was re-born with a new identity.

ERLING: God always seemed alive and near to me when I was a boy. I never had to ask for his presence. He charged the very air around me, and I could always reach out and touch him. When I learned later that the Holy Spirit is called the "wind" of God, I knew that I had experienced that as reality long before I could describe it. He was the sunlight, the gladness, the gaiety, the security of the atmosphere about me. I didn't need the proof that Marge had asked; I just knew he was real, and that made me feel real, too.

Maybe it was partly because my home was next to our church, separated only by a hedge and fifty feet of grass. The life of that small town congregation flowed around me, and its worship life brought almost all of the community right by my home. I spent so much of my time with the family of God that met there.

At Christmas time especially I seemed to experience a spiritual rebirth. The angels and archangels and all the company of heaven took shape for me in the sharp whiteness of moon on high-piled snow. The crispness of 40-degree-below-zero weather, the crunch of snow underfoot as we carolled, the music of the God who came wrapped up in flesh marks my spirit with the sweet memory of those childhood Christmases even now.

The darker side of memory recalls the man who drove too fast and crashed into a ditch just a mile from town. The inscription on his simple wooden casket in the small single room mortuary just a block from my home said "Rest in Peace." I pondered that phrase. From what I knew he hadn't discovered peace in his restless life. That fact bothered me and forced me to come to terms with who I was in relationship to the God who was so real to me.

Sometimes I'd visit my cousins in their farm home

surrounded by fertile fields of grain. On Sunday we'd go by horse and buckboard to worship at the country church which stood in the middle of a graveyard. Walking among the graves, I recognized names of people whose lives had touched mine. Would I really see them all again in the world to come? My answer was always a believing *yes*.

The realism of God's presence through the life and death of that small community powerfully influenced all of my growing years. I reveled in the fact that I was baptized into the name of Jesus, that God loved me, and that I had meaning. I wanted to spend my life for and with God.

The crystallization of those longings came when I was 14. Our confirmation class review came on one of those nose-pinching cold winter nights. The pastor asked many questions, testing our knowledge and commitment to the words of the Scripture and of the catechism, and I felt the seriousness of trying to give the right answers.

At about 10 o'clock I walked out of the warmth of the church fellowship into the cold world lit by the full-orbed Dakota moon, and completed my commitment to God in the confirmation of my own heart. The choice of vocation didn't matter except that I said, "My life is yours, Lord. You grab it and use it as you please."

Why was I so conscious of God as a child? Why do my memories seem so laden with the whole idea of his presence? Was it an illusion because of something in my home life?

My memories of home are generally very pleasant, but dominating all of them is the memory of my father's stern quietness.

As a young man he had come from Norway to follow

the railroad west to Maddock, looking for work. When he arrived in that tiny settlement, he was already a skilled housepainter, known for the daring spirit that made him unafraid to climb to the top of the tallest house and even to paint the needle-pointed tower of the white wooden church.

After five years of working and saving, he sent for Gunhild, the gentle young woman, ten years his junior, for whom he had come to seek a fortune in America. For Gunhild, the cold Dakota prairies must have been a disappointing contrast to her beloved Gudbrandsdalen, and I wonder if she ever really forgave Ole for bringing her so far away from that mountain valley home. But she bore her new life patiently if not enthusiastically, enduring it as young Christian women of that day were taught to do. The rigors of bearing and caring for seven children eventually forced her into semi-invalidism, and young Norwegian immigrant girls came to "live in" and help care for the family.

Housepainting did not provide enough support for a large family, and dad later worked hard as the manager of a grain elevator and seller of coal, all of which enabled us to live very well in that small town. One of my greatest joys was being invited to work with dad at the grain elevator and to help unload boxcars full of coal, but he was not at all vocal in expressing his love, so it was hard to feel close to him. His convictions were definite, and he was closed to any unveiling of his inner feelings. I craved his affection and wanted so much for him to put his arms around me and to say, "I love you."

I sensed that he had hurts, too. Some of the bitterest memories of my childhood are the years he drank too much. Then his daily homecoming was an event to dread. Even when I was older, those years were to stay a dark and forbidden area of family life, locked to any discussion.

Fear revives even these many years later when I recall at least one night when my father poured kerosene on the coal in the potbellied stove in our living room and the flames leaped up. We were all very frightened, but when we tried to stop him he became very angry. Memories like that can never be erased, I've learned, even though when I was 15 years old he stopped drinking completely and remained a model of sobriety for the rest of his life.

Whatever longing I had for a father's expressed love I found in the God whose assurances of love for us "children" found a response in my heart.

I feel that in some ways we were all the poorer in my family because we were not encouraged to talk about our feelings. Our whole religious experience was basically an intellectual one. That's not all bad because a religion based *only* on subjective feelings is also one-sided. But the truth is that we behave according to our feelings and then use our minds to rationalize those actions. We are really ruled by our feelings whether we like that or not. What a tragedy that we can't talk about these forces that are so important in our behavior and have such profound effects on our sense of who we are and our relationships with each other.

REFLECTION EXERCISE

1. Look at those early sections of your lifeline. Mark your earliest memory. Usually it's associated, as were ours, with feelings of fear or guilt or rejection.

To be free to make choices which are not chained by the traumatic experiences of the past, there at some time must be a fearlessly honest exploration of memory and *an appropriation of God's grace in the healing of our memories.* To experience that healing, do your utmost to let your own love bathe those toward whom you feel bitter for the wrongs—real or imagined—which they did to "ruin your life." Can you tell them about your feelings and the love you now feel?

To break the power of the past to control our lifelines, we must claim it as our own, without shame or rejection, without judgment, and let its positive learnings give us strength to live in newness of life.

2. What events from your past have given positive strength to your identity now? Explore the feelings that rise within you when these events are visualized in your mind.

3. Continue to rejoice in them as they bathe you with feelings of blessing.

3.

How Do You Feel?

"How do you feel?" we ask so casually without really wanting an answer. Yet the answer to that question reveals so much that's significant in the management of our lives. Just think for a moment of how many of our decisions are affected by the way our body feels. A headache may ruin a speech, lose a sale, alienate the family, and change all your carefully made plans for the day!

When people are faced with the choice of moving, the climate of the new area becomes a very important consideration in the decision to move or to stay. A body that shivers in every cool breeze that blows may rebel against a decision to move to a place where temperatures fall below zero for much of the year. Parts of our country are really "hell" to someone who cannot stand hot weather! Delight in warm winters may quickly wilt in six months of unbearable heat. The body *does* influence the management of our lives.

ERLING: With some lingering effects of my paralysis, I know that my whole feeling about myself has changed. When I was able to move freely and walk with a spring in my step, holding my head high, I felt confident and in charge of myself. I liked my body and its sense of well-being. I felt attractive and drawn to other people. Now I wonder how effective I am, and I tend to project onto others my feelings of not liking myself when I hurt physically.

At times like that, when inhibiting limitations compress me, I think, "This is really another person's body and I've been transplanted into it! The Erling Wold who used to move so easily, who shoveled tons of coal as a boy and tossed 100-pound bundles of hay, died in the ocean, and his spirit now resides in an alien body."

Since body and spirit interact so intimately with each other, damage to either one affects the other. Until I lost the physical powers I once had I didn't realize how many decisions we make very easily when our bodies function well. Now I have to think through plans, decisions and choices much more carefully. Even though the invitation to go to Taiwan last spring came to both me and Marge, I reluctantly made the decision not to go with her because I felt that I could not endure 17 consecutive hours of sitting in planes and buses and waiting rooms. In the spirit I wanted to go and be part of that experience with Marge but my body refused to cooperate.

Daily the struggle goes on to be happy with my body now and to really accept it as my own. I think that the fact that I've managed to do that at all has come through the rejoicing in the abilities I *do* have rather than concentrating on those that I've lost. But it's almost a daily need to reclaim this present body as my own.

In other less obvious ways, the appearance of our body influences our life decisions. In our culture, our physical appearance may be the first standard against which we measure ourselves and others. The person who is grossly overweight has a difficult time with acceptance of self and the development of an adequate self-image. Anyone who has suffered a crippling or scarring disease will be influenced by that fact. A young man may choose not to play basketball even though he has every other quality needed to do well in the game, simply because he is afflicted with a severe case of acne on his back and arms. Rejection of one's own body may engender feelings of self-hatred that affect emotional well-being.

ERLING: One recent summer two newsmen for a national magazine put an attractive used car on the edge of a road near a large city. Leaving it there unoccupied, they sat in seclusion some hundreds of feet behind it with a camera focused on the scene. In mere moments a family came by, noticed the parked car, braked their own car, and then backed up to it. As if they had planned for it, the father came out with the necessary tools and removed the radiator. They had scarcely driven off with it, when another group came and took the wheels. Even the knowledgeable reporters were shocked by the speed with which the car was totally stripped. Finally a group of children broke all the windows. The reporters published a sequence of pictures describing the fate of the car.

Now, at times, I feel that I am that car. I permit so many destructive forces to victimize me. My physical condition makes me vulnerable for some people to strip me of my sense of self-worth and to leave me feeling less than I really am.

Al (a fictitious name, of course) does this to me. Whenever I meet him, I always leave the encounter feeling depressed. There's something about the way he comes at me that I just cannot handle constructively. He seems to specialize in nit-picking and expressing opinions that reflect his own negative perceptions of life in the church and especially of people in positions of leadership. Even though I recognize that he's projecting his dissatisfactions with his own life on me, I fall helplessly into his web. I've watched him at work on others, too. His self-esteem seems to feed on destroying the integrity of other persons, and my own defenses go up when he approaches.

I don't need Al to make me feel inadequate. Like many others with physical disabilities I struggle daily to maintain a sense of personal worth and the power to live significantly.

One of the reasons we have such a difficult time liking our own bodies (and therefore our selves) is because our society places such a high value on persons who fit its standards for physical "perfection," and those standards are at odds with the real worth of persons.

Check yourself: are your first reactions to others likely to be influenced by their physical appearance?

If you have ever worked with groups of children—especially in a preschool setting—you have observed that it's the "cute" youngsters who draw most of the unsolicited attention from staff members (if they're not careful), and these children certainly elicit comments from other parents. The little one with tumbling curls and classical baby features gets the pats on the head and hears remarks like, "Isn't this a darling child?" The parent's own child may be within earshot and, hearing that involuntary comment, immediately concludes, "I must be ugly. No one ever says that about me! My mommy and daddy wish I looked pretty, too."

40

There's just no getting away from the fact that we value people first of all because of the way they look and perform physically. The performance of the child who is able to ride a two-wheeler at the age of four wins the admiration of the neighbors. Just count the number of times your affirmations of others take the form of compliments about their physical appearance. Check your own reactions to the child who's not "cute" and the one who is.

In addition to such general reactions, we are really at a loss to know how to react to those who are suffering from obvious physical handicaps. As one young woman who has had arthritis since adolescence said, with some bitterness, "When you have something wrong with you physically, people treat you as though it affects your mind and all your senses, too. I've had people say right in front of me, 'I wonder what's wrong with *her*?' as though I can't hear them or have no feeling about what they're saying."

Handicapped children are likely to find their handicap the chief topic of conversations they overhear between adults. We have had many children in our parish nursery schools who were born with inadequate hearing or partial blindness and have noted that other parents and teachers focus all their remarks to the parents of that child around the handicap. What were they doing for it? What was the prognosis? How did the child feel about it? How did the mother feel about it? And so on. The child, if he or she is within hearing distance, becomes well aware that that physical condition is going to be the most determinant factor in life for her or him.

MARGE: The only boy I remember from my 7th-grade class is Louis Malek. I don't remember any of the other boys' names. I remember some of the girls because they stayed friends through high school, but Louis I can see in my mind's eye a score of years later—and I have never forgotten his name. Much as I might *like* to forget both him and his name, Louis is associated in my memory with a physical feature which figured largely in my own self-concept in those adolescent years. Louis sat to my right about three rows away in the days when even 7th-graders sat in straight rows at nailed-down desks.

Every time I turned to the right and saw Louis Malek, he would outline on his own generous profile a very large nose!

Now because Louis himself had a nose which could hold its own with some very famous ones, he realized that my adolescent nose, at that time probably the dominant feature of my face, was a sensitive object in my own self-image. Louis managed to raise my consciousness of its size considerably, to the point where I would sit with my hand over my nose whenever I thought someone was looking at me from the side. Strange, isn't it, that one boy could do that to one person and make me forget that I had two good eyes, two good ears, four workable limbs, and all the marvelous intricacies of body that God gives to each one of us and forced me to concentrate on the one thing that he had decided was my "handicap"!

For this reason young people feel totally destroyed if they have such normal adolescent "problems" as acne or are too short to make the team or a head taller (especially girls) than anyone else in the class. They have a hard time believing in their own worth no matter how delightful they may be in every other respect.

For men, after adolescence, society changes its evaluation of their worth. Unless the boy becomes a professional athlete or enters a profession, such as acting or modeling, where physical appearance is a prerequisite for success, physical strength and beauty take second place to intelligence. No matter how good-looking a man may be, unless he can perform successfully in his business or profession, he will not make it.

For women there is no change in the demand to be physically attractive throughout their lifetime. Women who come to be counseled for feelings of depression often identify their depression with the way they look: they're getting too fat, their wrinkles are showing, they look too old. Appearance is equated with sexual attractiveness, which is also required of women by our society.

Television reinforces stereotypes for all of us, but certainly for women. Every woman held up as an "ideal" woman has thick lustrous hair, smoothly unblemished skin, never wears more than a size 10, and, even though grown children appear with her, she herself is never over 35 years in appearance! Is it any wonder that the American Medical Society has identified the most likely candidate for suicide attempt as a 35-year-old married woman with two or three children?

ERLING: During the months after my hospitalization when my depression over my physical condition was most acute, Marge encouraged me by telling me that now God was giving me an opportunity to develop my "inner energies," something I had never really taken time to do in the days when every moment was given over to physical energies. In my former *outward* wholeness, I had neglected much of my *inward* wholeness. Our hope lies in helping our children and ourselves to develop a true sense of values, one that is not based only on outward appearances. Not easy, but Jesus demonstrated a new set of values.

Even in the Bible there seems to be a drastic change in the way persons are described in the Old and New Testaments. In the Old Testament people are often identified by physical characteristics, such as King Saul being more handsome and a head taller than the other men around him (1 Sam. 9:2); Rebecca being "very fair to look upon" (Gen. 24:16); Rachel being "beautiful and lovely" (Gen. 29:17); and Esther becoming a queen because she won a beauty contest (Esther 2:2-4).

But in the New Testament we never find one reference to the fact that Jesus called anyone into his service on the basis of physical or mental criteria. We don't know whether his followers—men or women—were short or tall, fat or thin, whether they learned easily or had learning difficulties; we don't know whether they moved with physical differences, or even how old they were. All we do know is that Jesus saw in each one a responsive heart, a willingness to do the will of God. His own mother, blessed above all women, is never described in any other way than for her moral purity and for her willingness to respond to God's will.

We do know that Paul suffered from a physical handicap all of his life—a handicap which he refers to as his "thorn in the flesh" (2 Cor. 12:7). That physical condition, whatever it was, definitely affected his spirit because, as he says, it kept him "from being too elated."

Discovering Jesus' lack of concern about physical appearances helps to free us from slavery to the world's value systems. We're not to conclude that Jesus *despises* the beautiful and the strong just because he does not single them out for special notice. That's an unfair assumption, because people beautiful by the world's measurements are just as much a possibility for discipleship in the company of Jesus as beautiful people by any other measurement. The phrase "Everything is beautiful in its own way," grips us with the enduring hope that some day we may begin to live out that fact in our own feelings and in our attitudes and behavior toward others.

On the other hand, if our physical appearance meets all of the approved cultural criteria, this may become such a source of ego satisfaction to us that decisions may be made only on the basis of bodily appearance and not on long-range goals which take into account the fact that physical appearance changes as one grows older.

If our body is not to be the determining factor in running our lives, then claiming it as part of ourselves, without either rejection or pride, becomes a freeing process.

Part of that process is learning to understand the message our bodies are constantly giving us through our five senses. There is also that sixth sense which is given to the Christian by God's Spirit, but first of all the task of human learning is to know ourselves through the impressions we receive from our bodily senses.

MARGE: I found North Dakota a great place to get in touch with my body. Always a person who is keenly aware of what I'm seeing, smelling, hearing and feeling, I don't even like to change the flavor of foods with a lot of salt. But North Dakota enhances physical awareness as no other place I've lived had done.

In the subzero weather I began to experience the limits of my own endurance and was constantly aware of wind blowing through my hair, of the numbness and pain of cold fingers and toes, and the sting of icy snow pellets on my cheeks. When the sun sparkles off the whiteness of snowdrifts the intensity of its brilliance is unparalleled by any other visual experience. Sight is impossible even with eyes narrowed to slits.

While I found North Dakota stimulating to the senses, I am not one of those hardy individuals who could get dressed in "long johns" and face mask and go out for brisk walks in the subzero weather. In fact, I got cold just listening to the daily weather reports—especially such announcements as the fact that the freezing time for unprotected skin that day was only 8 seconds! I used to marvel at the little children who spent hours on the outdoor skating rinks.

Much of my exhilaration came from looking out the window at the kaleidoscope of seasonal changes. Most winter days I would wake up to bright sunlight spraying powdered-sugar trees with gold and mirroring itself in a million airborne ice crystals. Snowbanks shimmered with virginal purity.

Unable to get outside for exercise, I responded to the changing landscape by putting a recording on or turning on the radio to music whose rhythms matched the mood of the weather. Sometimes I'd sit with earphones on and let symphonies of sound bathe my psyche; at other times I was compelled to move around the room (no way can I dignify that movement by calling it dancing!) to the melodies pouring forth. One day our son came home early from high school and, unaware of his presence in the loudness of the music, I "danced" on. When I saw him and stopped in embarrassment, he simply said, "Don't stop. I have to leave now but I'll catch the rest of your act tomorrow!"

Think what you will about such antics, but it's still

good for me to feel aware of the presence of God through the functioning of my own physical being.

Between us, Erling and Marge, there is a wide variation in bodily function: Erling fighting partial paralysis and Marge still enjoying her abundant physical energy. Nevertheless, each one of us claims our body with all of its own familiar scars and markings and bumps and aches as part of our wholeness. We do not want to live alien to our own physical feelings.

Unless I explore and claim my physical feelings, I only half know who I am; or maybe I don't know myself at all, because my physical self is all I can actually see when I look into the mirror or see myself reflected in the mirror of another's eyes. It's like living in a house that may have many things wrong with it and still being able to say, "It's a good old house. It's *my* house. I like it and I feel comfortable here. I know where the worn spots are; I know its sounds at night and which boards creak. I claim this house as my dwelling place. If I moved away, I'd miss it."

The invasion of this physical world by the Son of God is the ultimate validation of our bodily experience. Jesus came in the flesh, not only so that we could know God in new ways but also so God could know us in new ways. Through this incarnation, he says to each one of us, "I am here to walk alongside you, to experience what you experience in your bodies, to know how they affect and reflect my Spirit within you. Not to judge that experience and not to deny it by avoiding it but to assume the same bodily form. And I'm going to walk in it exactly the same way you walk in it, without special privilege or exemptions. I'm tempted just as you are, suffer just as you suffer, feel rejection as you feel rejected; I am hurt and broken as you are hurt and broken. The only difference will be that I'll show you the light at the end of the tunnel. I'll transform the scream of your physical pain into hope, your physical death into resurrection, your illness into health, your brokenness into wholeness, your alienation into reconciliation!"

What an adventure for the Son of God! His own fascinating intelligence, possessing the mysteries of all the eternities, was captured in human flesh, fenced in with all the restraints of a human body. And then he didn't even get recognized for who he really was (John 1:10)! We hunger for appreciation; Jesus knew that hunger and went unrecognized by his own people. We want to be thought "beautiful"; Jesus was despised as ugly and rejected by the very ones he came to save from the ugliness of sin. He knew all the pain of being human.

Jesus pitched the tent of his own flesh next to ours and chose to be our brother. He knew thirst, hunger, loneliness, pain, and terror. As a sharer of our daily life, he sought no more status than to live as one of us. The Apostle Paul wrote about this fantastic subjection in the words, "Have this mind among yourselves, which you have in Christ Jesus, who, though he was in the form of God, did not count this equality with God a thing to be grasped, but emptied himself, taking the form of a servant . . . (Phil. 2:5-7)." That servant form was the shape of a human body.

Though he accepted himself as fully human, he shares with us the secrets of living a more abundant human life. Above all, he shares the obsession with death that afflicts all of us who are aware of our inevitable dying. In an interview with John Dart, religion editor for the Los Angeles *Times,* the comedian Woody Allen talked about his obsession with death. He never escapes from it; it's with him wherever he goes. "I think it's the only important question. And until more light is shed on death, if possible, all the other questions people are obsessed with can never be fully answered. . . . I think ultimately that is what everybody is writing about, or worrying about. It's the key issue in human life." Allen says that he is hoping for a very "up" answer, that there is an afterlife, that death is "not some total end."

Jesus shared that fear when he cried in the Garden of Gethsemane the night before he died, asking God to take away the fearful crucifixion he was destined to endure. The humanity he chose took a toll on his spirit, too.

In the voluntary acceptance of a human body, Jesus recreated our flesh, spoiled by sin and the ravages of physical vulnerability, into a temple of the spirit. He accepted his fleshly form as a gift from the body of a young woman and gave it back to each one of us transformed by his spirit. He so ennobled the human clay that all of his followers are urged to give their own bodies in the same way he did, as "living sacrifices," because they are, through him, wholly acceptable to God —no matter what their shape, appearance, or IQ. It's our *bodies* that are members of Christ and belong to the Lord, their value being the price of his own body on the cross.

The ultimate honor accorded the body of our flesh is to share in the Lord's own resurrection. He raised his own human body out of the grave, and, as a result, we who bear the same earthly image as he shall also bear the image of the imperishable body which he made possible (1 Cor. 15:42-50). This flesh in which we live is the seed from which the resurrected body takes its form.

In Greek mythology, there is the story of a Trojan

priest named Laocoön and his sons who, because they warned the Trojans against the wooden gift horse of the Greeks, were attacked by two enormous serpents sent by the infuriated goddess Athene. In a famous sculpture of this wretched family, one can see their bulging eyes and their tensed muscles convulsing in their attempts to break the hold of the tightly coiled snakes.

Unlike them, our Lord, Jesus Christ, chained with us in the coils of human flesh, reclaims his own body and ours from the stranglehold of Death.

Like our Lord, we can say with pride, "This is my body! I claim it as my own, in glory and in pain, in the same sure and certain knowledge of its present value and ultimate resurrection."

REFLECTION EXERCISE

1. How do you feel about your body? Some cannot stand to look at their own body in a mirror for fear of the feelings its image arouses. What messages does your body give you? Do your feelings about it have anything to do with the way you saw yourself reflected in the eyes of your parents or in the eyes of your teachers? Your classmates? Your peer group now?

2. What messages about yourself do you get from advertising? In what ways does the physical appearance of others affect your judgments about their value as persons?

3. Do you have a "thorn in the flesh"? What does it do to you? How have you received enough grace to live with it? How has it affected your "reasonable service"?

4. Practice standing in front of a mirror saying, "This is my body!" Say it four times, each time stressing a dif-

ferent word. Claim its uniqueness as you have claimed your own lifeline and your own past.

5. Are you taking care of your body? Do you give it enough rest, get enough exercise, eat the right foods?

4.

What Choice Do I Have?

MARGE: The South Side Express was unusually crowded when I started home some time after 10 o'clock. In the days before the Chicago subway the elevated trains provided the fastest and cheapest cross-city transportation. After we reached the Loop, I transferred to a Logan Square "L." Since all seats were taken, I had a long night ride clinging to a swaying overhead strap.

People were sleeping in the seats, mouths falling open and heads jerking dangerously. *I'd be sleeping too if I had a seat,* I thought resentfully.

The train was picking up speed; heads jerked against other heads and their owners wakened, gave each other dirty looks and were soon sleeping again. *We're really making time tonight,* I thought, trying to keep my footing as the train rocked down the track. The rocking motion increased, and some of the sleepers began to wake up. People began to look around uneasily, muttering about the excessive speed.

"What's the hurry?"

"Where's the fire?"

The door at the rear of our car opened and closed

quickly, but in that brief moment the loud machine gun-like click of the speeding wheels made my pulse quicken. A uniformed trainman pushed his way between us to the other end of the car, ignoring the questions and curses of the frightened passengers.

On his way, he kept saying, "Stay in your seats! Everything's under control!" Then the door at the front of the car opened, letting in another quick burst of machine gun-like clicking and the trainman was gone.

The train was obviously *not* in control, speeding dangerously on its 3-story-high trestle. A few screams mingled with the curses and mutterings, and a child began to cry. No one was sleeping now; mothers held small children tightly; couples huddled together; a man who had been monopolizing a stationary pole silently offered me part of it to hang on to. Noisy curses gave way to silence. Someone was saying the rosary. All I could think of was the power rail and how it might feel to fall on its millions of volts.

Unexpectedly, the train slowed down and proceeded at normal speed. The release of tension brought crying, laughing, jokes, pretense, and instant camaraderie! My own legs began shaking, and I would have cried except that I wanted to be cool.

People are still suffering from the earthquake that awakened all of us in the Los Angeles area at 6:01 A.M. on February 9, 1971. A diagnosis of incurable cancer, a broken neck in an accident, living through a disaster—all of these seem to call forth those feelings of helplessness and anxiety.

"Out of control!"

That's the message we've gotten from so many. A shared sense of being victimized by hostile forces paralyzes us. "What's the use of doing anything if you can lose everything you've lived for in one moment? Why try at all?"

A massive epidemic of powerlessness makes us prey to easy answers and simple solutions.

Prophets of doom and destruction capitalize on our fears. Religious quackery runs rampant, and charlatans get rich exploiting our helplessness. "Experts" arise on every side, claiming to explain those forces which appear to be playing a chess game with human lives. Identified as demonic or angelic, the spirit of Satan or the Spirit of God, these forces bypass the human will.

We have had people tell us that they were, to use their own words, "zapped" by the Holy Spirit, as though they had made no previous choices that might have led to their special experience. "The devil made me do it," becomes a convenient excuse for denying the choices which lead to a particular action. Some play the role of puppets jerked about by Whoever or Whatever pulls the strings that move them through life.

"Do I have any choice?"

The Christian's answer to that question is a resounding "Yes!" The power to choose, that function we label the "will," is a gift from our gracious God. The power to choose separates us from all other creatures.

The creatures who inhabit Aldous Huxley's *Brave New World* are to be pitied, but not only because a totalitarian figure determined their "role" in that world long before they were born by decreeing which chemicals were to go into the jars in which their embryos were forming. Their tragedy lies in the fact that they have been convinced from birth that they do not *want* to make any choices contrary to those that are made for them. They are, in fact, without *power* to make choices!

All of us react in horror to the thought of brain surgery that can reduce humans into will-less robots, but how often have you talked to people who say that they really have no choice in their own situation?

The most miraculous of human functions is the ability to choose, but because the "will" holds the key to human behavior, it becomes the prize which many would like to capture and control. From their first encounter with the tempter in the Garden of Eden, human beings have been the objects of intense pressure to yield their wills to the control of someone other than God.

One of our sons, who worked as a marketing research analyst, told us of the intensive training he received in methods designed to motivate people to buy things they really didn't need, or even *want*, to buy. Subtle pressures are applied to control buying behavior: the way products are packaged, their placement on shelves and in display areas, their location in the floor plan of a store. Slogans are used to play on hidden fears, on guilt associations, and on basic human needs.

An organization to help people lose weight warns its members to be aware of the traps merchandisers set which cause the dieter to buy food items she or he does not need. Members are trained through "awareness exercises" to understand that advertising methods are designed to make profits for the store owner and not to meet the best needs of the customer. Being aware of these commercial pressures helps the buyer resist purchasing articles which are unwanted, unnecessary, and even harmful.

Television commercials control the will with the subtle suggestion that the buyer of the advertised product will have a happier life, appealing to a basic human desire. Buy this, and your spouse or children will love you more! Use this product, and life will be worth living again!

Because they know which "buttons to push," demagogues are successful in leading masses of people into behaving contrary to their own value systems. Hitler knew that the fear of communism was a powerful ally on his behalf in the promotion of a world war and in forcing a nation to make choices which were really against its will.

All varieties of human engineering and behavior modification seek ways to negate or bypass the human will. While the reinforcement of desirable behavior is a valuable tool in the learning process, in the hands of someone whose value systems are contrary to our own behavior, modification is inimical to our best interests.

The will should never, for instance, be yielded to unqualified or incompetent hypnotists. Amateurs who claim to know something about the subject are dangerous. The integrity and the credentials of the hypnotist are always to be questioned. We know and recommend some very fine therapists who use hypnotism in competent ways to facilitate the therapeutic process, but we also know the dangers when hypnotism is used by manipulators. Most states require licensing for persons who use hypnotism in clinical practice.

Some of you may even be aware of the ways mass hypnotism is used in "religious" gatherings for the purpose of controlling behavior.

Then again, we are aware that it sometimes suits our conscious or unconscious needs *not* to have any "willpower." We play the "zombie" part. Instead of "The devil made me do it," we simply say, "I don't know *what* made me do it." We hear statements like this when someone tries to explain why he has uncontrollable fits of anger and beats his spouse or children. "I just don't know what came over me," he says.

Or the person who weighs much more than he or she should and says, "I don't know what came over me, but I went to the store and bought two pounds of candy and ate it all." Of course, we all have a dark side in our nature, from which unconscious impulses arise even against our will.

But we *choose* to be out of control at other times because then we need not take responsibility for our own actions. We can simply say to ourselves, "It really wasn't me that did it."

MARGE: It helps me to realize that I have some power to choose my way even in the areas of life for which I have assumed I have no choice.

One day a woman called for help with the tearful sob, "If this keeps on much longer, I'm going to crack up!"

When we met I asked her, after she had made the same statement again, "*When* are you going to crack up?"

That, of course, upset her a little.

"Well, how do I know *when?*"

"I heard you say you were going to crack up, if your situation remains as it is now. That sounds to me as though you've made a decision to crack up, and now it's just a matter of deciding when things are bad enough to do it."

"Well, I really don't *want* to crack up! Who'd want that?" she asked, looking as though she wondered why she had called me.

"What would you *rather* do?" I tried again.

By the time we had explored alternatives to "cracking up," she at least was aware that there were other choices she could make before "choosing" to crack up.

Her husband had chosen to leave his family as his way of avoiding responsible behavior; she was going to choose having a nervous breakdown as her way of getting out of all the responsibilities which had suddenly been placed on her. Both were irresponsible choices.

Before we go on, none of this discussion of choices will be very helpful unless we clarify what we mean by being *free* to make choices.

How "free" are we? Even though the words "freedom" and "liberation" have a very contemporary ring, they bring a long history with them. For theologians the question of "free will" provokes much debate. Is the free will really free? How free, and in what areas? Where does God's grace enter the picture?

Before checking the theology, let's look at the idea of freedom of choice in its broader dimensions.

We find helpful a study by Mortimer Adler, director of The Institute of Philosophical Research. In a two-volume work called *The Idea of Freedom: A Dialectical Examination of the Conceptions of Freedom,* Adler and his associates examine the ideas on freedom represented in the works of more than 100 leading Western thinkers. They arrived at three broad categories of freedom:

1. Natural freedom

This most widely recognized type of freedom is common to all people, regardless of race, sex, or place of origin; nor is it dependent on our moral condition or our purposes. "To be or not to be," to eat or not to eat, to deny desire or to act on it—these and other questions involving alternatives are the areas in which natural freedom of choice is exercised.

2. Circumstantial freedom

While we all possess a "natural" ability and freedom to choose, circumstances often dictate whether or not we are able to *act* in a way which will enable us to *realize* our choices. The political situation in which we live, legal restraints, physical disabilities, climate, poverty, imprisonment—these and other circumstances affect our freedom of operation. Our current liberation movements take place because of societal, cultural, theological, and political restrictions on the freedom of minorities, women, and of the aged.

3. Acquired freedom

Not natural to humankind, the freedom to live beyond self-interest is "acquired" as a gift of God's grace, enabling us to live the life of moral goodness.

For Christians, acquired freedom identifies what Jesus was talking about in John 8:32 when he says that those who continue in his word will know the truth, "and the truth will make you free." In Romans 8:2 we read that "the law of the Spirit of life in Christ Jesus has set me free from the law of sin and death," and this is the freedom proclaimed in Galatians 5:1, "For freedom Christ has set us free!"

Conversion of the will is the basis for any freedom to make choices consistent with God's will for all creation: "because the creation itself will be set free from its bondage to decay and obtain the glorious liberty of the children of God" (Rom. 8:21).

Have you been "born again?" Jesus says in John 3:3-5 that this is absolutely necessary for all of human life if our will is to rise beyond self-interest, circumstances, and the passions and hostilities that work against our own good and the good of others. Just as we have all been born as children of fleshly parents—unique and individual—so we must be born again to live out our unique and individual lives as children of God. "For the mind that is set on the flesh is hostile to God; it does not submit to God's law, indeed it cannot; and those who are in the flesh cannot please God" (Rom. 8:7-8).

Even though we have horizontal relationships in the flesh, they are subject to the destructive hostilities that alienate us from God. Because we cannot love God without being born again, neither can we love ourselves or those around us as we ought. We are lost in self-hatred that explodes against ourselves and others.

In a small midwestern town we spoke at a meeting where two families were present who had not spoken to each other for 18 years. Before that they had been good friends, but one night the son of one family and the daughter of the other were on a date. The boy was driving the car and collided with another vehicle. The girl died, and because the boy had been drinking beer before the accident, her parents never forgave him. For 18 years the parents of the two young people had not spoken to one another, but had stayed in the same church. While this is a more dramatic situation than many, think of all the hostilities that divide us from one another.

The will that is reborn can still choose hostility, but it also has the freedom to make choices consistent with God's love, the kind of love which chose to love us "in that while we were yet sinners Christ died for us" (Rom. 5:8). John Ylvisaker has written a song with the theme, "That's the thing I don't like about Jesus." Many things we may not like about the demands of obedience to our

Lord, but the will that is "re-born free" is set on pleasing God and not the demands of our own flesh.

The possibility of a will freed from the bondage of sin and death begins with a cry in the heart like that of the jailer at Philippi, "What must I do to be saved?" (Acts 16:30).

Every day becomes a re-enactment of the new birth experience when, waking to the newness of the morning, we rise again from the womb of night, to mercies that are "new every morning" (Lam. 3:22-23).

In all cases there comes a time when conscious commitment is made to the Lordship of Christ. The born-again will decides to subject itself to the will of God. For both of us that time came in adolescence; for some it is part of a natural developmental process (as in Erling's case) and for others the experience duplicates the agony and pain of physical birth all over again (as for Marge). In any case God's Spirit works the gracious work in our hearts, opening our eyes to see once-hidden mysteries.

The Apostle Paul's experience dramatizes the behavioral changes that separate the person whose will has been "converted" from its natural state from the person who has not experienced the new birth. Acts 9:1-31 records Saul's adventure on the way to Damascus, where he was going to persecute and murder Christians. On the road to Damascus the Lord Jesus Christ appeared to him in a vision of light and asked those searching questions which eventually changed Saul into a disciple of Christ named Paul.

In the process, he was made blind and a man named Ananias, in obedience to the Lord's command, laid hands on him and restored Saul's sight. "Something like scales" fell from Saul's eyes, and those who had known him as a persecutor now witnessed a remarkable change in his behavior, a change compatible with Paul's description in 2 Cor. 5:17, "Therefore, if any one is in Christ, he is a new creation; the old has passed away, behold, the new has come." That new behavior possessed the following elements, and you might want to test your own "newness" against them:

1. A new identity

In Paul's case, his name was even changed from Saul to Paul. The behavioral change is most apparent in those whose previous behaviors were most obviously destructive to themselves and others (for example, murderers, drug addicts, alcoholics, or sadists), and is evidenced even in physical appearance. They look different; they act differently; there's a complete change of personality. Paul was obviously not the murderer that Saul was; but no matter what our previous history, others should be able to observe a change in our behavior, because our will is set free to make new choices.

2. A new outlook

Something "like scales" falls from our eyes. Like sleepwalkers who wake up, we see clearly rather than in a dream. Paul reworks an old pagan saying in a Christian context in Eph. 5:13-14 where he writes, "Awake, O sleeper, and arise from the dead, And Christ shall give you light." People will often say after a renewing experience, "The sun shines brighter; the grass grows greener; the roses smell sweeter; children seem more lovable; neighbors are friendlier." Life is seen through new eyes!

3. New relationships

Relationships have a way of sorting themselves out without conscious effort on the part of the "new" person. People who were formerly attracted to us may shy away now. People to whom we were attracted may now repel us, and we find ourselves responding with a different kind of "love" for them. We care about people we never cared about before and are even moved to fight injustices against them. Paul, the gentile-hating Pharisee, becomes the apostle to the gentiles, following Jesus' "peace" ministry of removing barriers that separate race from race and class from class.

4. A new purpose

Our list of "wants" becomes different. Our changed wills are headed in another direction. If before our dream was to have a million dollars, we may still have that dream—but for a different purpose (if our new will decides that it really wants to expend its energies in the accumulation of wealth!) The jobs we assume along the way may change, but the direction of our lives points in the direction of the purpose God has in mind for our lives.

5. New conversation

All of the old conversational topics that intrigued the old identity are called into question. If we were caught up in our own emotional and physical ills before, we may be opened to "love your neighbor as you love yourself." A young woman who had experienced a "new birth" at a retreat told of being freed from loneliness to reach out to others. Formerly, she had waited for others to reach out to her, even making it difficult for them by hurrying home from church and isolating herself in her apartment. She found so many new things to talk about outside her preoccupation with self. Others may find our new conversation tiresome if they have not shared a similar experience; somehow that doesn't seem to matter because we find others who are eager to share our newness.

6. New likes
Books, movies, TV, activities, food, drink, the Bible—all of these are seen in new ways and sort themselves according to new likes and dislikes.

7. New meanings
Words are invested with new meaning: brotherhood, sisterhood, family, society, church, love, joy, peace, faith, hope. Check your vocabulary and note how it has changed.

8. New pain
Loneliness may be a by-product of the new birth experiences that follow the rebirth of our will under God, because these propel us out of the traditional spheres in which we formerly found our associations. Whenever we experience a change of identity or outlook and adopt new behavior patterns, we are out in a void where familiar faces and meanings are absent. Jesus said that following him involves cross-bearing and being hated as he was. We can also expect the pain of rejection and loss.

The newness begins with a changed inner consciousness—what the Bible calls the "heart." Unless the heart is changed, there is no way to effect a permanent change in behavior. Rules won't do it. No one has ever lived the Ten Commandments perfectly. No moral and ethical system will change the world through the self-determination of its adherents. Standards against which goodness can be measured will not guarantee the performance of piety. *A change in the direction of the will is a work of grace and not self-determination.* Imposed legalism, without inner confirmation of the "heart," sooner or later causes emotional conflict because the behavior it demands is at odds with the unregenerate will.

The new birth is always both an event and a process. Beginning with baptism, its dynamic quality engages us in daily birthings—eye-opening, identity-changing, often painfully growing experiences. God's Holy Spirit daily renews, enlightens, and sanctifies me, and each day I am born again to newness of life.

Daily I am set free to choose between life and death, hope and despair, love and hate, patience or irritation, anger or self-control, humility or pride, acceptance or rejection.

Do you have any choice? God says "yes"; what do you say?

REFLECTION EXERCISE

1. Have you ever felt "out of control," the victim of forces seemingly not subject to your own will?

2. What events in your life have produced such feelings?

3. In what ways are you experiencing natural freedom? circumstantial freedom? acquired freedom?

4. How does being "born again" affect your day-to-day choices? your relationships?

5. If you have any question about what it means to be "born again," talk to a pastor or a trusted Christian friend. Read John 3.

5.

What's God's Will for Me?

Wherever we have talked about the will of God, we've always sensed a sparking of interest. Eyes light up, people lean forward in their chairs, bodies reflect an eager expectancy, questions keep coming: "Is there a 'will of God' for *me?* How can I know it? How can I possibly do it?"

We know that we have a lot of hungers. We want fulfillment and a sense of wholeness. The hunger for security gnaws at us. We long to love and be loved. We need fun and celebration. But under all of these needs and drives, the born-again, grace-restored human will longs to do the will of God.

To arrive at an understanding of the answer to our question, "What's God's will for me?" we must face the fact that the real question is, "*Whom do you want to serve?*"

When we step into the newness of life with Christ, when resurrection has replaced death, when singing has replaced mourning, and joy has dissipated the fog of despair, we want celebration and dancing, transfiguration and glory. Away with gloom and sadness, long faces and dark robes! Bring out the fatted calf, make a merry feast, and let the bands play on!

Do we dare bring into this festive atmosphere the word *servanthood* and *slavery?*

Our own experience is that it's very easy for us to follow Jesus in the "glory" aspects of his life—to run with the Palm Sunday crowds, to climb the transfiguration mountains. Speaking at conventions, preaching Sunday sermons, giving testimonies before crowds, talking about the "gifts" which God has given us, publishing books—all of these are "glory" experiences. Of course, one must sweat through preparations of talks, through the writing of books, through committee and board meetings, and a lot of mundane drudgery, but the talks and the books and the testimonies all bring their rewards.

Where we have trouble with the will of God is in an area of the *risk* involved in its performance. The risk is that it costs me my life. We are called to a life of total submission to the will of God; there are no halfway measures, no part-time employments.

The serving of God demands the obedience of a slave.

MARGE: I was privileged to be a speaker at a retreat in Squaw Valley recently with a woman who has her doctorate in theology. Totally blind, she has as her constant companion a German shepherd dog named Jeanie.

One of the discussions at the retreat focused on the concept of servanthood. I commented on the fact that this beautiful dog pictured for me exactly what it means to be a servant of God, a slave of Jesus Christ. The dog's will is totally subjected to Harriet's will. The dog lives with only one purpose in mind—to take care of Harriet, to protect her, to go where Harriet wants to go, to deny any of her own wants in order to serve Harriet's wants.

Nothing else distracts that dog from her devotion and duty to her mistress. The relationship between Harriet and her dog is unbelievably beautiful, and one can sense a total merging of personalities in their relationship.

I talked about Harriet and her dog to another woman who was familiar with the training of "seeing eye" dogs and she reported that the dog undergoes a period of real confusion when it is re-assigned from the trainer to the new owner. During the training period the trainer demands absolute allegiance from the young dog. When the new and permanent owner comes into the dog's life, the trainer must reject it, and that results in a period of disorientation for the dog until its will is retrained to serve the new owner.

Jesus said, "No one can serve two masters; for either he will hate the one and love the other, or he will be devoted to the one and despise the other. You cannot serve God and mammon" (Matt. 6:24).

To do the will of God means to yield oneself as a slave, totally possessed, totally under the orders of the owner. That concept of being a slave to God or, if you prefer, a servant of God, runs through both the Old and the New Testaments. In the Old Testament, the word for servant is the same as the word for slave and means a totality of submission—not in any compulsory sense, however, but in a willing yielding.

Do you recall the child Samuel who heard God's voice in the temple and responded, "Speak, for thy servant hears" (1 Sam. 3:10)? King David called himself a servant of God. When the devil came to ask God for the privilege of testing Job, he identifies Job as God's servant. Mary, the mother of Jesus, described herself as God's servant, wanting to do whatever God willed.

The profoundest concept of servanthood is that of the devotee lost in worship of the revered one, oblivious to self-concerns, caught up in adoring service. In the Revelation that service is described, "Therefore are they before the throne of God, and serve him day and night within his temple; and he who sits upon the throne will shelter them with his presence" (Rev. 7:15).

Before you rebel against God as a demanding taskmaster, recall that you are in the service of One who has acted on your behalf long before you have given anything in return. Before Romans 12:1 calls you to present your body as a living sacrifice in reasonable service, the word "therefore" presupposes everything that has gone before in that letter to the Romans. The entire 11 chapters prior to that verse tell of the mercies of God toward us. Read the marching promises of life in Christ through those chapters: "For the wages of sin is death, but the free gift of God is eternal life in Christ Jesus our Lord" (Rom. 6:23); "There is therefore now no condemnation for those who are in Christ Jesus. For the law of the Spirit of life in Christ Jesus has set me free from the law of sin and death (8:1-2); "We know that in everything God works for good with those who love him, and who are called according to his purpose" (8:28).

The call to full surrender comes from a God who has acted on our behalf throughout history. Even before asking the Israelites to keep the Law which came to them on Mount Sinai, God reminds them that "I am the Lord your God, who brought you out of the land of Egypt, out of the house of bondage."

Therefore *serve*. Because of what God has already done for you. You *choose*. "I call heaven and earth to witness against you this day, that I have set before you life and death, blessing and curse; therefore choose life, that you and your descendants may live, loving the Lord your God, obeying his voice, and cleaving to him; for that means life to you and length of days" (Deut. 30:19-20).

Obedience to God and servanthood are unpopular concepts in a world with the slogan, "Do your own thing." In fact, the world seems to be dedicated to tyranny rather than to servanthood. Controlling *others* seems to be the mind of our time.

Just as nations surrender to dictatorial regimes, even the church falls prey to this need. Because we need to have people "under" us, we fabricate all kinds of structures where we can control other people's lives. We devise systems where "orders of authority" rule; we organize ranks of "disciples" who are set under an "authority" who controls their actions. Even among Christians, under the guise of serving God, the old unconverted will tries to promote its self-seeking concerns by deriving *authority* from God rather than *servanthood*.

These are all to be seen for what they really are: devices of our sinful nature to "muscle in" on God's territory. All of us are ultimately responsible only to God and not to any other authority. The very first commandment calls for only one allegiance. But the subtle temptation of the serpent still comes with the suggestion that there is a way in which we can "be like God" (Gen. 3:5). There is only one authority to obey, and the apostles put it very bluntly when they responded to the priestly authorities, "We must obey God rather than men" (Acts 5:29).

Pastors cannot determine for their parishioners how each one shall perform his or her servanthood; a wife cannot determine for her husband what form his service to God must take; a husband cannot dictate to his wife the way she shall spend her life in obedience to God. Each one must answer to God for the way each life is lived. To play God in another's life is to play a game where the stakes are another person's eternal destiny.

Authority and power over others are the antithesis of the Christ-life. Jesus found it necessary to repeat this many times to his disciples. "And he sat down and called the twelve; and he said to them, 'If any one would be first, he must be last of all and servant of all'" (Mark 9:35). He warned them not to play the "authority role" of the Pharisees when he told them "You are not to be called rabbi, for you have one teacher, and you are all brethren. And call no man your father on earth, for you have one Father, who is in heaven. Neither be called masters, for you have one master, the Christ. He who is greatest among you shall be your servant; whoever exalts himself will be humbled, and whoever humbles himself will be exalted" (Matt. 23:8-12).

So the "authority"-commissioned persecutor named Saul, converted by the grace of God in Christ, sums up the meaning of that conversion in 1 Cor. 9:19 when he says that though he has been made "free from all" he has made himself a "slave to all."

We are called to *voluntary* servitude to God. *That's God's will for every life.*

How, and in what ways, you perform that will in *your* daily life becomes a matter for *your own* new will to decide.

MARGE: I was all set to sit down at my typewriter for an entire day of work on this book. The nice clean square on my appointment calendar looked potentially productive, reserved especially for book writing. I had even planned not to answer the phone in the event that my thoughts began to flow freely. Today, I thought, I won't let myself be interrupted by anything that's extraneous to my writing.

However, before I could get started, the phone rang at 7:30 in the morning. Thinking that anyone who called that early must have something urgent to say, I answered and was immediately caught (trapped?) by one of those situations which mean a whole day spent (wasted?) in helping another person. In such situations I find my thoughts doing some swift calculating: "I have really *important* things to do today. I'm an author, I've got a book to write with a deadline pressing. Don't I have a prior responsibility to the publisher? Besides, even if I didn't have the book, I have other 'important' things that I should be doing. I'm conducting a retreat this weekend and I have four talks to prepare for that. Hundreds of people will hear me there; isn't that more important? Now here's this call from only one woman (we'll call her Tess) who needs a ride to the doctor with her two-month-old baby. The baby has been in the hospital; they're on welfare; their car broke down; her husband is out of work and is sick and on medication."

As the story unfolded over the phone, I was faced with a quick "servanthood" decision: does someone who has really *important* things to do take time out to share the burdens of someone who obviously is going to be in some sort of trouble all her life?

I had known Tess from previous times. She was the one who called me at 5:30 in the morning to talk for an hour because she can't sleep at night—especially when her right palm itches because then she knows something bad is going to happen that day! She has been on welfare for a long time (deservedly so); she was married before and her first husband (6 feet tall and 230 pounds) has come and beat up her second husband (5 feet 8 inches tall and 150 pounds); her mother rejects her but constantly hassles her; her father lives in Iowa and won't communicate with her; her brother told her to "get lost"; etc., etc., etc.

You all know someone like Tess, and we suspect that their needs are never going to be resolved either emotionally or physically, and it's easy to rationalize yourself out of helping because of that conviction. Besides, we say, Tess and her husband are probably the kind of people who will never be able to stand on their own two feet and have gotten so used to asking others for help that it's become a way of life for them.

All of this may be perfectly true, and, just as quickly as information whizzes through the small electronic components of a pocket calculator, these thoughts went through my mind. Nevertheless, either because I'm a "sucker" or "I feel guilty when I say no" or I've been conditioned to being a helper, or maybe—just maybe— the Spirit was testing my commitment to servanthood— I knew that I just could not say no to Tess.

So instead of working on the book, I spent from 9:00 in the morning until 2:00 in the afternoon taking Tess and her baby to a doctor, waiting in that office for an hour and a half, taking her over to another doctor who was supposed to do surgery on her foot since she had cut it twice on broken glass. He sent her over to another doctor (I never did figure that one out) to get a letter certifying something about her condition. That doctor's secretary said she'd get the letter ready by 3:30 but not a minute sooner. (I learned something about the way folks on welfare get victimized by "red tape" and their own dependencies.)

I took Tess and the baby home thinking I might wait

in her apartment with her until time to get that letter. When we got there, we found that her husband had been able to get the car fixed and, "if they had gas money," they could get to the doctor themselves. So I handed them a couple of dollars for gas money and know, just as surely as I am writing this, that it won't be long before Tess will call me again, either in the middle of the night or during the day and some other crisis will have arisen in her life.

Even though we have learned from decades of experience in the ministry that we are perpetually being "conned" (as are hundreds of other people), we have made a conscious decision that this does not really matter. The important thing is to follow, as nearly as we can determine, in the steps of Jesus, who came not to be "ministered to" but "to minister" and freely gave himself to the needs of the deaf, the maimed, the blind and the poor, without any hope of reward and often without a word of thanks.

To do these things for the sake of "feeling good" about ourselves is unrealistic. Resentment may be a more real feeling at times! We do them out of obedience to our Lord, the new owner of our wills, who said, "A new commandment I give to you, that you love one another; even as I have loved you, that you also love one another. By this all men will know that you are my disciples, if you have love for one another" (John 13:34-35).

Despite many cults and self-appointed prophets who preach that prosperity is the right of every Christian and that God's blessing is a life free from problems, we cannot find anything in the Scripture to substantiate this. One has only to read the Gospels to find that Jesus did not promise a bed of roses or a life of ease. Instead he walked the dusty pathways of Palestine without a place to lay his head. James, the brother of the Lord, warns against the temptation to give preference to the rich person in the congregation over the poor person (James 2:1-7).

It's only too true that the demands of high office often stand very much in the way of person-to-person ministries and form a barrier to personal contact with the "little ones" of the earth who were so precious to Jesus. Our occupations as professional church workers open many opportunities for personal ministry to us, but sometimes they also limit us. Administrative positions in church or government often separate people from the very constituency whose needs they are trying to meet.

As the number of "Tesses" in our world multiply, we are increasingly faced with the dilemma of programming services to people for the sake of efficiency and at the same time maintaining the effective personal touch. With a program organized to listen to the cries that come from every quarter and to respond quickly to the needs they represent, our efforts can be multiplied many times.

The danger lies in relying solely on the impersonality of organized efforts to respond to human need to the exclusion of personal ministry. Imagine someone directing efforts to feed the victims of famine overseas and at the same time never seeing the starving children in her or his home town! The story of the rich man who never paid attention to the beggar at his own gate warns us of the same oversight. The parable of the Good Samaritan does not direct its lessons to people intent on doing evil but to church professionals who had no time for person-to-person ministry.

Turning Tess over to a professional agency was a possibility. We have "hotline" volunteers and social service volunteers available. But sometimes you know that *you* are the one singled out for a particular ministry and the Spirit will not permit you to turn away from it. The decision is yours; you can't escape by letting someone else make your decisions about ministry for you.

Ministry is another name for service. God's calling for every life—without regard for the distinctions of sex, race, age, physical or economic condition, or occupation—is *servanthood* or *ministry*. The performance of one's ministry transcends all of the traditional, cultural, and ecclesiastical barriers which may seek to limit it for any one of us.

One of the associates of Dwight L. Moody, A. J. Gordon (1836-1895), pastor of one of Boston's largest Baptist churches for over 25 years, tells the story of a brilliant woman named Adele Fielde who was recalled from China by her mission board because her senior missionaries accused her of "preaching" and thus transcending her sphere as a woman. When the charge was read to her, she described the immense area she served in China —an area where she, with a native woman, had gathered groups of men, women, and children together and proclaimed the gospel of the cross.

"If this is preaching, I plead guilty to the charge," were her words to her examiners on the board.

When she was asked by them whether or not she had ever been "ordained" to preach, she replied with dignity, "No, but I believe I have been *foreordained*."

The call to be "ministers" comes to every follower of the Lord and to him we are responsible for the way in which our ministry is lived. "You were bought with a price; do not become slaves of men" (1 Cor. 7:23).

We are set free to serve one another. Occupation and ministry are not the same thing. One occupation can open more opportunities for ministry than another; but there's no occupation that closes one to ministry. Ministry means responding to the needs of those about us in the name of Jesus Christ, and those needs exist wherever people are. They cry in the executive suites of corporations and the assembly lines of factories; they lie with patients in hospital beds and walk the rounds with medical staffs; they sit next to us on planes and come knocking at our doors; and *everywhere* we are called to "bear one another's burdens, and so fulfil the law of Christ" (Gal. 6:2).

Sometimes people bring their needs to churches and the professional staffs who are available there; more often they turn to the "ministers" who live and work beside them.

MARGE: When we were very small children we used to play a game called, "Frank, Frank, he's killing me!" The game grew out of a weekly and sometimes semi-weekly drama played out by the people who lived next door to us. The husband was a nice, jolly man—except when he stopped at the tavern on his way home from work and turned into a "Mr. Hyde." Then beating up his wife became his favorite sport. She would play her part in this recurring domestic tragedy by leaning out the window of their upstairs flat and screaming across the narrow gangway that separated their dwelling from ours those lines which became the basis for our game, "Frank, help me! Frank, he's killing me!"

Faithfully, whenever his name was called, my father responded by going next door to try and calm our raging neighbor. If his efforts were ineffective, he came home and called the police. That always heightened the excitement of the drama for us children, especially if we had already gone to bed, because then we could open our window a little and listen in the dark to the deliciously frightening violence next door.

But I'm not telling this to indicate any heartlessness on our part (because children often use drama to work out their own fears of such violent scenes), but to emphasize the fact that my pa, tired from his own long work day, never failed to respond to the needs of our neighbors. Sometimes it was with a sigh that he put his shoes back on when the call came, but as he said, "What else can the poor woman do? Who else can help? I'm right here."

Our neighbors would never turn to a professional minister for help, but they felt free to call on my parents for ministry.

Making choices in our servanthood priorities is no easy matter. Is it a matter which can be settled in terms of numbers? The greater the field, the more valuable the service? The larger the church, the more honor due the leadership? The higher the office, the greater the servanthood?

The study of Jesus' own ministry does not reinforce such judgments. His ministry was primarily to and with *individuals;* numbers appear irrelevant. Those who pressed close to him called for his immediate response.

Those who are closest to us appear to be our first priority for ministry—parents, children, spouses, friends, our own congregation, our own community, our own place of employment. Priorities change with age and place. Parents caught up in ministry to a young family may search for new areas of service when those children are grown.

But never is there any exemption from ministry. The

circumstances of our birth and early life may affect our ministries; the condition of our bodies may shape our choices; but none of these factors exempts us from the day-to-day struggle to make decisions for servanthood.

We sometimes hear wives say, "My husband won't let me do that." Or we hear husbands give the excuse, "My wife takes care of religion for our family." The mature Christian takes responsibility for servanthood-choices. Perhaps the eagerness with which we permit others to assume such authority over our decision-making represents a flight from servanthood, a way of rebelling against the call to the obedience which belongs to the Lord alone. It's easier to let someone else *tell* us what to do than to struggle with our own decision-making.

But it's also very dangerous. God calls each one to account for ministry. That's God's will for each life.

REFLECTION EXERCISE

1. Am I seeing all the opportunities for ministry around me?

2. What, in my life, might *legitimately* keep me from responding to a call like the one that came from Tess? What might *not* be valid reasons for deciding not to respond?

3. Is there a program you can become involved in which will give you more opportunities to minister effectively to the needs of others?

4. Why is it sometimes easier to be a member of a committee that administers helping programs than it is to deal personally with those who need ministering?

5. How do you avoid responsibility for decision-making when faced with choices for servanthood?

6. What are some ways you may be avoiding ministry?

7. Is it necessary to feel guilty if you must say no at times? Where do you think those feelings come from?

8. When we say in this chapter that everyone is called to ministry, does that have a freeing or a binding effect on you? Or both?

6.

What Makes Dreams Come True?

Nothing happens in this world without a dream in someone's heart: a dream of the kind of person I want to be, a dream of the kind of life I want to live. Whatever we do starts with a dream in the heart.

Capturing a dream, or a vision, for your life of servanthood—a dream that's your very own—that's the first step toward any goal.

A recent letter from a young woman had this paragraph in it: "I've spent much of my life making decisions which I thought I *ought to* make. I'm working hard at changing this. Rather than deciding what I 'should do' I'm trying to decide what I 'want to do.'"

This young woman, a college student, wrote to us not in a spirit of rebellion or the desire to live a totally self-centered life but out of an agonizing search for her life goals. At the age of 25, she realizes that she is one-third of the way through her expected lifeline. She doesn't have any profound inner urge to give her life to any one particular occupation or profession.

Some young people seem to know early in life what they want to do. Unless some crisis changes their plans, they go through life on a road without detours. Their "dream" may be to discover the cure for cancer, to make a million dollars, to be on the first flight to the moon, to have a happy home—but whatever that dream is, they seem to know early the goal toward which they are going to bend all their energies.

For most of us the ability to state clearly what it is we want out of life is not that easy. Yet until we can complete the sentence "My dream is . . ." with an enthusiastic conclusion all our own, we are apt to flounder around and feel dissatisfied with our life.

A fascinating phrase from Psalm 37:4 comes to mind: "Take delight in the Lord, and he will give you the desires of your heart." For years we thought this meant that God would do what we ask of him when we found delight in serving him. That's true, but the profounder realism that runs through the promise is the fact that even the desires (dreams) that are created within us are put there by God.

Then *how* do I make my dreams come true?

1. Find your dream and believe in it.

In your new sense of self-esteem as one who is loved and accepted by God—with your own unique past and present, with your own particular body and background—you can believe that your dream is as valid and worthwhile as anyone else's.

But you have to identify it. How do you complete the statement, "I want . . ."? Maybe you have more than one want (dream). Go ahead, make a list.

No one else can determine our life goals for us. How many people do you know who confess that they've never been happy in the work they're doing; that they feel their lives are being "wasted"? Yet if they were to do it all over again, many of them say, "I don't know what I would do differently." They've never been caught by a dream of their own.

One of the problems with putting dreams or wants down on paper is that they may represent only those things that we can agree to with our intellect but which do not find confirmation in our feelings. Writing things down is a rational process, but our behavior comes out of our feelings.

It's hard to say just how many young people we've known who've started college with the desire to be a teacher. Perhaps because they had some good teacher "models" when they were growing up, or for some other reason, they decided on teaching as their profession. Since the academic preparation for most professions is really a "head trip," most students do not experience the "feelings" of being a teacher until student teaching starts. Unfortunately that frequently doesn't happen until their last year in college, at which time they discover that they can't stand the classroom situation and dislike working with large groups of children.

Our list of wants must be *ours,* not only intellectually, but also emotionally. Duty, responsibility, and law may enter into our dreams, but they must also give us a sense of delight, fun, and worth.

Ask yourself as you check your list of wants: Do I feel this is the thing I *ought* to do? That I *should* do? Or does it come out of my own feelings of *wanting* to do it? Is it really *my* dream or is it someone else's dream for me?

Much conflict is avoided if the dreams of parents for a child happen to coincide with the child's own dreams, but that frequently is not the case. One of the dilemmas parents face is the question of how to help children make decisions and choices. The temptation is to make choices for children long after they should be making their own choices and learning the technique of decision-making. One of the ways this can be done is by providing good models for children as they are growing.

ERLING: Even though Lester Lieth was my earliest hero, perhaps that wasn't all bad! At least he was a defender of the oppressed and a helper of the poor. Later I saw my pastor in much the same light, only as a more realistic model in terms of my developing relationship to Jesus Christ.

MARGE: There were two women who captured my imagination. The first was Marie Sklodowska, the Polish girl whom the world knows as Marie Curie. She was the discoverer of radium and freely gave the results of her work to the world without holding back and with no thought of monetary reward. How I longed to live in an unheated garret in Paris and dedicate my life to a calling as demanding as hers!

The second model for my life came later in the person of Mary Slessor, the Welsh factory girl who answered the call of the Lord in her life by going alone to Africa. In the lion-infested jungles of Calabar, she labored fearlessly to bring the people there to her Lord. I knew I could never be that courageous, but she gave me courage for lesser tasks.

One of the big questions facing all Christian parents is how to direct the child's will so that it will learn obedience to the will of God without making that child so subject to authority that *anyone* can come in to her or his life and take control.

After many years of involvement in the preschool

training of children, we have come to believe that those parents most likely to rear children who can withstand peer pressures and resist authority figures who want to control them in harmful ways are the parents who enable their children to make wise choices on their own.

Of course, this training must be begun when the child is ready for it, and that depends on the individual child. In any case, begin with choices between two alternatives and not with such wide open choices as, "What do you want to wear today?" In the nursery school, choices are given in this way, "Do you want to play with puzzles or paint?" Not, "What do you want to do now?"

The result of parental discipline and training should not be will-less little robots who obey every parental command without question, but thinking individuals who are trained to make their own wise choices in life even after they leave their parents. When children are faced with decisions, parents can help them investigate alternatives and examine the responsibilities involved in their decisions.

When the decision is made, the parent must be willing to let the child "own" the final decision, even allowing the child to learn by failure. Without the right to fail, there is no freedom of choice. To do only what the parents want may in the long run mean failure for the child, who will not be able to withstand the authority of any parental figure who places him or her in a childlike position later in life.

Because they have not been helped with decision-making and given practice in making their own decisions, many young people from homes with concerned parents come under the influence of rigid authority figures such as those who ruled the Children of God, the Manson Family, and the Symbionese Liberation Army.

Women are especially vulnerable to this dangerous possibility because our early cultural conditioning of girls often emphasizes their subjection to males. Sociologist Lewis Yablonsky of California State University at Northridge believes that Patty Hearst and Lynette Fromme acted in such a robot-like manner. "With no definite ego of their own, they placed themselves in a totally subservient position following orders. They have low or no self-esteem, and they are desperately seeking recognition and approval."

To be able to say out of one's own allegiance to God, "I have a dream . . ." is the first and perhaps the most difficult step in all achievement.

MARGE: I still have dreams of my own. We need to challenge the old song that talked about the day "when I grow too old to dream." For God's people that day never comes. The Spirit keeps dreams fresh and new.

Just this year I have been caught by another dream. I am convinced that some of us who have demonstrated that it's possible to survive 3 decades of marriage and still enjoy our lives together while maintaining individual identities must find ways of sharing that experience with others.

My own commitment to this will take shape in more graduate study in the field of marriage and family counseling. As a Christian, I believe that I have some special contributions to make, but I also need the skills which more study will give.

If claiming our own "dream" is the first requirement, then the second step toward making that dream come true is:

2. Be willing to suffer to make it come true.

We never had to live in an unheated garret like Marie Curie in order to make our dreams come true, but some of the places we lived were almost that bad! Our first church was a mission which we started ourselves. In those days no house was furnished and there was no church or office equipment. There were no packaged missions then, and we had to start from scratch. That meant living in two rented rooms in the home of an elderly couple in Fort Worth.

That house has now been torn down, probably because it was condemned! Returning from our one-day honeymoon at a Dallas hotel, we unpacked our wedding gift sheets and blankets. Just as we turned out the light, we heard a familiar scratching sound from the couch in the other room of our "furnished apartment." In our first week there, we killed nine mice! Neither one of us had ever seen a cockroach before, but soon learned what they looked like. We loved Texans, but never did get used to scorpions and tarantulas!

Our second home was in the same building as the "church." We had three rooms in the back of the one-storey stucco building which was remodeled to house our growing congregation. The word *privacy* had no meaning for us during this period of our lives.

Now I doubt if we could stand some of the things that were part of our life then: the poverty, the pressures to get a church going and at the same time meet people's needs, three babies not many years apart. But we've all gone through times like that to make our dreams come true.

Without a willingness to endure hardship of one kind or another no dream is ever realized, no vision brought to reality.

ERLING: I never knew what it was to suffer for the sake of a dream until I thought I'd never walk or work again. When I lay in that intensive care unit totally paralyzed, having to be fed and washed and without any control over my bodily functions, I was consumed by a dream of wholeness. I dreamed at night of walking, of hugging my children, of touching Marge; my days were motivated by the thought of moving again.

But I recoiled from any touch on my body. Unbearable pricking and tingling accompanied every contact with another object or person, and any time my arms or legs were moved during nursing routines, I experienced pain and muscle spasms. I dreaded therapy sessions, and at the same time I looked forward to them with eagerness because I knew they were my only hope for movement and the realization of my dream.

We wrote the story of my dream come true in our book *What Do I Have to Do—Break My Neck?* and through it have been permitted to share in the sufferings of others caught up in their own dreams of wholeness.

There's "Mama" Miller of San Diego who lived three days without knowing that her neck had been broken when she tripped over a rug and fell against the edge of a door. "I broke my neck at the age of 77," she writes, "and the doctors shook their heads because I wasn't dead or paralyzed. But I didn't know my neck was broken even though the pain was terrific, because I've lived with so much pain for years. I drove 600 miles to visit my son before going to the hospital. I am a living example of the power of God—The God Who Is Enough!"

I was called to see John, the high school athlete from Glendale who broke his neck in a dive at Ventura Beach. His dream is to be a counselor. Strapped in a wheelchair because he can't move either arms or legs, he is pushed 3 blocks to Glendale City College to study for his degree.

Then there's Dan, our friend the helicopter pilot whom we mentioned in *Thanks for the Mountain.* Dan's now in Washington state where his wheelchair is no handicap as he testifies of God's mercies to anyone who will listen —and even to some who won't!

We met recently with a group called "High Hopes" in Newport Beach, an organization which has become a support group to the hundreds of parents in the beach area whose sons and daughters wage a never-ending battle with the crippling effects of brain and spine injuries. "High Hopes" is the by-product of the dreams of Lee Merriman, whose son was told after a brain-stem injury that he would be a *vegetable* (I hate that word!) for the rest of his life. Lee wouldn't believe it and dedicated herself to making her dream for him come true. Today, 2 years later, 19-year-old Mike is attending Orange Coast College! And "High Hopes," organized by Lee and others who prayed and worked with her to make Mike live a productive life, is there to give hope to all who live with "impossible" dreams.

Maybe in this great country of ours we have lost some of the capacity to suffer for our dreams. As we move into our third century of national life, we'll be remembering the hardships that our pioneer forebears endured. We'll pay tribute to those who died in order that civil and religious freedom might live in our land, people like Mary Dyer who was hanged for daring to practice her Quaker faith in Boston. In those years the Puritan clergy held not only religious but political power. They were afraid that the Quakers would pervert people from their own "true" religion so they had laws passed forbidding anyone to practice any other religious faith. In order to challenge that law, Mary Dyer deliberately moved to Boston from the freedom of Rhode Island. On May 21, 1660, she was brought before the governor of the colony and refused to leave under pain of death. On June 1, 1660, she was hanged, but a year later, because of her example, others spoke out against the cruel laws and they were repealed.

Around our world today people are still being imprisoned and tortured for their faith and dying to change oppressive civil and religious laws. We may never be called to that kind of suffering, but in a lesser degree anyone who stands up for his or her convictions understands what those others are enduring. As we rejoice in the freedom to implement our own dreams, how willing are we to share the suffering of those who are forbidden by circumstances from implementing theirs? Maybe the only kind of "suffering" we in the United States are able to share now is the pain of parting with some of our savings to help alleviate suffering around the world.

The dream of many for enough food to eat, pure water to drink, and the opportunity for education can never be realized even with the willingness to suffer. Sometimes only the shared suffering of others who are "willing to bear one another's burdens" in a servanthood ministry is going to make a difference.

Suffering alone won't make the dream come true. You must also:

3. Work out a plan for making it come true.

You've got your list of dreams or wants. Now put each one at the top of a separate page and underneath list all the things which you need to do to realize that dream. As you list them, you might even come to the conclusion that the dream is unrealistic. Perhaps it would take too much money, too much time away from the family, or it would ruin long-standing friendships. Only you can decide how realistic your dreams are. While you want to "dream the impossible dream," you must also be realistic enough to recognize that it may be unattainable. But you may also decide that it's worth trying and that the fun will be in the effort.

Maybe you just need to explore more options. That's where others can help you see the larger picture when you are stuck in examining only one section.

What needs to be done first? What's the order of importance? Making lists helps some of us divide our time into manageable segments of activity. Reaching larger goals is simply a matter of many smaller activities successfully completed, each one a step toward the final goal.

Allot time to each activity on your list. How many hours or days are you going to set aside for this one or that one? If you work best under pressure, then cut the time short. If you go to pieces under pressure, then allow more time for each task.

When we sigh, "I'm busy all the time, but I never seem to get anything accomplished," it's usually due to one of two things. Either we don't think our activities accomplish anything because we don't see a "pay off" in them. Or we really do expend our energies in a lot of undirected activity.

In his book *Love and Will*, Rollo May defines will in one sense as "*the capacity to organize one's self* so that movement in a certain direction or toward a certain goal may take place."

MARGE: It's in the management of my daily time that the whole question of "Who's running my life?" comes into focus for me. There I've learned that the telephone too often runs my life. More than any other single factor the telephone *demands* time. Very few people can resist the compulsion to answer the phone. But on some days, in the interest of other priorities, I begin the day by warning myself, "Do not answer the telephone today. Let it ring. It doesn't own you. It's in the house for your convenience and not to dominate your life!"

I need to tell myself that—that the telephone cannot preempt time that I've committed to other tasks. One of my regrets as a mother is that I didn't write this on my calendar earlier in my life: "Don't answer the phone when you're playing with the kids!" I recall one of my children saying to me, "How come you told me you didn't have time to read me a story, but you talked so long to that lady on the telephone?" Very early I should have learned that the phone can be the foe of important priorities. For family members and friends you can arrange a time to talk which is convenient for both of you.

Television cannot demand time the way the telephone can. Your own hand reaches out to turn that appliance on. It doesn't turn on by itself but as the result of a conscious choice on your part. The phone rings without our asking it to and it rings insistently and demandingly. I know it takes a strong effort of my will not to answer it.

Of course, we have to allow for emergency distractions. You can't program for broken legs or stopped-up plumbing or vacationing relatives or visiting dignitaries, and somehow we have to develop enough flexibility to meet such interruptions without going into a state of shock.

Sometimes, in the interest of honesty, we have to admit that we *want* distractions. Whenever we are faced with starting a book, for example, we can find all kinds of ways to keep from starting. We sharpen pencils, hunt for a pen with just the right kind of point, go to the store for a new typewriter ribbon, make a cup of coffee or tea, decide that we should eat early to give us more uninterrupted time later—the list is endless.

Self-discipline makes us use time in the interest of our priorities. Have you learned that time is the most important gift we have? Once it's slipped into the past, it can never be recalled. Only you can decide in your life what chores can be left undone in the interest of larger priorities. We've learned to live with snack meals, dust, unread magazines, and postcard correspondence. What you'd *like* to have must be balanced against what is *necessary* if you want to realize your dreams.

Using the old "When-you've-eaten-your-meal-you-can-have-dessert" approach, we try to get the things we like least done first. That's a self-imposed form of discipline that works for us.

There's one area in which self-discipline is a necessity for most of us "workaholics." That's in the need to:

4. Have fun while making your dreams come true!

The need to have fun is basic to every life, as basic as the need for love and a sense of self-worth. Yet our work-ethic background often prevents us from acknowledging and acting on this fact.

How many marriages break up simply because they're no longer fun? Even making love has ceased to be fun and has fallen into that duty category that must have afflicted a lot of Christians in Corinth, motivating Paul to warn husbands and wives to give each other their "conjugal *rights*" (1 Cor. 7:3). When the marriage relationship stops being fun, it's due for some help.

How many people break down simply because they no longer enjoy living? Why not stop right now to ask yourself, "Am I having any fun in my life? How can I include that in my planning? What occasions do I have for wholehearted laughter?" What does it take to make you enjoy life?

If you're caught up in a dream, working toward making it come true can be all the fun you need, but a break in routine usually makes us more productive. The kind of "dedication" to a task once applauded as ideal has been found to be less productive than dedication balanced between work and play. Many companies are now insisting that their employees use up vacation time even when they don't want to. For some stimulating thoughts on work and leisure, read Gordon Dahl's *Work, Play and Worship*.

One day we forced ourselves to take time off from some strenuous, last-minute, beat-the-deadline writing to sit on the beach, just smelling the fishy saltness of the ocean, listening to the booming of the waves, letting our minds wander with the seagulls as they nibbled their endless snacks from sea and sand. For a long time we were quietly absorbed by the way the gulls "repackaged" their wings every time they landed. That one picture was so renewing that we returned home ready to record all the other thoughts that started dancing across our minds because of that one provocative image. Maybe watching seagulls fold their wings doesn't do for you what it does for us, so you need to find your own way of having fun!

ERLING: There was a time when the most refreshing break in my working schedule took the form of physical exercise: cutting the lawn, playing tennis, running. Now many of my withdrawals from reality take the form of "fantasy breaks" which are similar to coffee breaks. I can lie down on the floor of my office for five minutes and just let my mind focus on some scene far removed from counseling appointments, correspondence, and newsletters. I can visit the Orient, where I spent several weeks on an Air Force mission to chaplains some years ago. I can walk through the lands of the Middle East in the footsteps of Jesus, just as I once walked them.

When I return to my office from that other scene, I find myself refreshed and ready to go back to work. While we are all aware that prolonged withdrawal from reality is harmful, we don't seem to understand that uninterrupted contact with reality for long periods is also harmful. I think it was Ray Bradbury, the science fiction writer, who said that the "ability to fantasize is the ability to survive."

I heartily recommend my fantasy breaks to students, executives, teachers, and all others who cannot leave their reality scenes physically but who can take mental breaks from their tasks. Even before my accident I found this an excellent way to survive preaching at three services on Sunday morning. (I have to confess that my floor-lying habit has caused some anxious moments for parishioners who have entered my study between services and found my body stretched out!)

The next time you need to "get away from it all," take a five-minute fantasy break. It's a relaxing (and cheap) way to go!

For all of you who depend on serendipity to make all your dreams come true, such as an unexpected bequest from a long-lost relative, winning prizes on a television show, or the offer of a job overseas, all of the above may sound too coldly and carefully plotted. But that's our next point.

5. Expect to be surprised in the way your dreams will come true!

We believe in working and planning toward goals, even doing a lot of sheer plodding, if that's what it takes. At the same time we've experienced some unsought and unplanned-for surprises.

MARGE: My experience on the mountain in Taiwan was one of those surprises from God in my life. Sometimes they come as direct insight, sometimes through friends, sometimes through reading the Word, and sometimes through nature.

One day I was trying to work out a talk on *partnership,* and it still hadn't "jelled" as I drove along the freeway to the place I was to speak. I glanced at a sign to see if my exit had come when right above the sign I saw eight small birds sitting on a wire, neatly divided into four pairs of two each! Alone in the car, I laughed out loud at this unexpected testimony of nature to the fact of partnership and went on my way certain that God had confirmed my choice of subject.

One of the reasons I learned to love North Dakota is the beauty of her skies. There I saw my first full-sky *aurora borealis,* where rays of light painted the vaulted heavens more beautifully than any Michelangelo could have conceived of doing. Every sunset was a spiritual experience.

But the most memorable occasion came one morning two months after we arrived. Those two months had not been happy ones. Both Thanksgiving and Christmas were the first holidays apart from our two older sons who were left in California colleges. I spent Christmas in a tiny hotel room in Rochester where our daughter was hospitalized. We felt estranged from all former associations and alone in a strange and unfriendly environment. In January I eagerly took an assignment in Minneapolis just to get away for a while from what seemed to me to be a bleak and frozen land with unfriendly inhabitants—a projection of my own feelings, I learned later.

It was still dark when Erling dropped me off at the Grand Forks International Airport, where I was informed by the ticket agent that the plane would be delayed 45 minutes before take-off because they couldn't get the cabin warm enough! The thermometer registered 30 degrees below zero that morning with a windchill of −70 degrees. I sat down in a row of chairs facing the eastern sky, where dawn was just beginning to appear above the flat, unbroken expanse of icy prairie.

Too sleepy to read or talk, I stared at that "wasteland." Then the sun rose—only instead of one sun, there were three! Three brilliant, blinding foci of light igniting the icy landscape into a blazing prairie fire! Excited and a little frightened, I called the attention of the woman dozing next to me to the phenomenon. She just said, "Haven't you ever seen sundogs before?" If I had, they had never looked like that. She informed me that they were caused by ice particles in the upper atmosphere and usually were a warning of colder weather to come.

I sat on the left side of the plane to be sure I could feast my eyes on those sundogs all the way to Minneapolis. To me they were signs that God's presence is everywhere, and they gloriously revived my dreams. My whole attitude was changed, and that place, dreaded for its strangeness, became one of the most exciting places I've ever lived.

God's surprising presence in enabling our dreams takes many forms. He has made himself known to us as a presence of light, as happened when Erling floated helplessly in the Pacific Ocean, and when our daughter Kristi was ill as a small child.

One of the most renewing surprises came to me in my own home in North Hollywood. Although I had long ago dedicated my dreams to the God I knew in Christ, I had known periods of intense anxiety about so many things during the years that followed that commitment—pressures over assignments, worry about the care of my five children, a sense of the inadequacy of my own commitment to God.

That morning in North Hollywood, alone in the house, I was for no accountable reason suddenly overwhelmed with a sense of God's goodness. A strong impulse to pray sent me to my knees, and words of praise such as I had never expressed before poured from my lips. An inexpressible joy bubbled over within my spirit, while at the same time tears rolled down my cheeks. With that experience in the Spirit came a new ministry, also, a ministry which has taken me into pressures more intense than anything I've known before, but still, even though more than ten years have passed since that day, the joy and freedom from anxiety remain.

Now I not only recognize with my intellect but I know in my emotions that all things are possible to the one who believes and that, through a will that delights in his service, God is the maker of dreams come true.

Dream your dreams and plan your plans and expect to be surprised with God's joy!

REFLECTION EXERCISE

In his book *Love and Will,* Rollo May tells about hearing Father William Lynch develop the thesis that "it is not wishing which causes [mental] illness but *lack of wishing.*"

1. What do you think he means by that statement?

2. How have you experienced that as a reality in your own life or the lives of others?

3. What surprises have you experienced from God as you've planned and suffered to make your dreams come true?

7.

How Are Big Decisions Made?

Before we thought of writing about this subject, we were interested in finding out how Christians made decicisions. We often asked people to tell us how they made decisions affecting their entire way of life. The answers ranged from, "I've never thought about it," to detailed management-by-objectives methods, to stories of "hunches" and visions.

When we became serious about the matter (mainly because we ourselves were in the process of making some important decisions for our own lives), we sent out the following questionnaire to people whom we knew had just made or were in the process of making life-changing decisions. The information we requested was:

1. How do you make decisions?

   Think of a recent specific situation in your life when you were forced to make an important decision. Describe the way you went about arriving at your final decision. In your answer, please consider the following points:

Bethlehem Lutheran Church
Two Harbors, Minn.

  a. Do you have a set process you use in all decision-making?
  b. Do you look for help outside of your own thought processes, as for instance, prayer, other people, circumstances, "fleeces," "signs," dreams, etc.? How do you use them?
  c. After you had made your decision in the specific case you have in mind, were you satisfied? Describe your feelings.
  d. What kind of evaluation have you made since then as to the "rightness" of your decision?
 2. Generally speaking, how do you feel about the way you make decisions which affect your life?
 3. What kind of helps do you think you need to make the decision-making process more effective for you?
 4. How do you think your decisions reflect God's will as you see it?

The people we addressed were all Christians by their own profession and that fact was implicit in their answers. The answers came by phone, by mail, in personal conversations, and by tape recording. We have selected three to share with you, feeling that they contain guidelines which have proved workable.

The first one is from a woman in her late thirties who was employed before her marriage in a medical profession. Her husband is also fully employed, and they have two children.

She writes the following in answer to the questions we asked:

 1. a. Not a set process, but I follow some general guidelines.

b. I look for help through 1) prayer; 2) consultation with others; 3) considering as many of the facts as I have available (pro and con); 4) taking the first step toward making the decision "happen" such as putting the house up for sale or going for the interview, etc.

In almost all instances when I've been asked to accept a new job at church or elsewhere, the thought has usually already occurred to me. These thoughts are usually very fleeting, almost subconscious, and as a rule I don't pay a lot of attention to them. At any rate, they're not enough to motivate me to actively seek the particular opportunity. If I'm asked to do something and I have had these thoughts, I consider this a "sign" and am usually favorably inclined to accept the new responsibility.

When we sold our other home and bought our present one, I considered it a "sign" when the buyers told us they'd bought their last home from people with the same name as ours, had exactly the down payment we needed, and offered a one-week escrow which fit beautifully with our needs at that time.

c. There is not always a complete feeling of satisfaction at first. It takes time to adjust to a new job, house, etc. It's hard to make changes and I think we're like most people in resisting this.

d. When I look back on the recent past, I can see how the whole picture fits together.

2. I feel good about the way I make decisions. I've always felt that if the particular decision didn't work out, I could always take an alternate course. Cou-

pled with this is my own self-confidence. The hardest part of making any decision occurs in the mind. I believe many people miss opportunities to serve due to a lack of confidence in themselves and are thus fearful of stepping out, taking the risk, that a decision requires.

3. I don't feel that I need any additional kind of helps in decision-making.

4. I just pray that if something is to be, then the right doors will open and that if it's not to be, the doors will be closed. If we truly believe that God's will is operative in our every day, then I feel we can be relaxed with a sense of anticipation rather than anxiety. There is for me a great degree of peace when I've prayed about a decision and then leave it in the hands of the One who knows my needs and talents better than I do.

This letter illustrates so well the fact that, without a feeling of our own worth and without faith in our own value as persons, decision-making is difficult. As she says, "The hardest part . . . occurs in the mind. I believe many people miss opportunities to serve due to a lack of confidence in themselves and are thus fearful of stepping out."

Someone else said, "Before you can manage anything, even your own life, you have to unclutter your mind." Check your feelings of inadequacy and the thoughts that drag you down. See if they come from the circumstances of your childhood, an inability to accept your own physical self as "beautiful," or the fact that you have never seen yourself as a loved child of God. Unclutter your mind by accepting God's evaluation of your worth. Then you, too, can "leave it in the hands of the One who knows my needs and talents better than I do." The writer, in confidence, doesn't say, "the One who knows *if* I have any talents," but assumes that she has talents.

A 40-year-old businessman, married, father of two children, writes:

> I'm going to answer your questions primarily on the basis of our recent agonizing decision to move across the country:
>
> 1. a. I do not have a set process that I go through in all decision-making. When you really think about it, most of your day is spent making decisions, but most are automatic or subconscious. Most important to me is the need to make decisions fast and not let them linger any longer than necessary. While I try to "stick" with decisions once they're made, I'm not afraid to change my mind if pertinent information becomes available that I might not have had when the decision was made.
>
>   *The Family.* For me, the *family* must come first. I considered the following questions: What would the move do to the children? Were they young enough and flexible enough to adjust to new surroundings? Was the location a good place to raise my family? Would my wife and I be happy in a new home, considering that we had been very happy in our last home?
>
>   I want to say that money was never a consideration. Had it been, we would never have made the move.
>
>   *The Challenge.* Was the job something that I

would enjoy and would it create a challenge big enough to keep me happy on the job? Would it be a step toward a still more satisfying career?

The Company. My company had been good to me for many years. In being selected for this new job, they were telling me that they felt I was most qualified to do something for them. Maybe this is odd in this day and age, but I believe both the company and myself have an obligation to each other. At first I said no to the offer, but when asked if I could suggest someone else, I realized that there was no one as well qualified as I for the job. So I simply changed my mind and said yes.

b. I do discuss major decisions with others. First and always with my wife and the other members of my family, with close friends, and I often have subtle discussions with people to find unsolicited answers.

Prayer is a part of my decisions and was of special importance to me in this decision.

c. I have always been satisfied with my decision. I try never to look back. This only tends to create insecurity and confusion. We try to avoid any judgments on our move for over a year, looking only at the positive aspects. We immediately got involved in the church here and that helped.

d. Today, less than one and one-half years after moving, my former position is being discontinued. I feel that I was led to make this decision.

2. I feel very good about the way *we* have been able to reach decisions. I am more forceful than my wife and make decisions faster, but when the deci-

sion affects us both, we work them out together and normally arrive at a good agreement.

3. I don't feel I need much help because I am forward and will seek advice and counsel any time it's needed.

4. I guess I honestly feel that our decisions do reflect God's will because we always seek His guidance and we have not been disappointed with the results. Perhaps the hardest decision we ever made was the one for my wife to undergo a necessary surgery that eliminated the possibility of children for us. But as you know we have since been blessed with two adopted children. How could we not feel that it was God's will for my wife to have her good health and still to have our children?

In his answer this man again demonstrates that feeling of confidence in his own abilities. Even though his job is in the business world, a strong sense of "ministry" comes through. Perhaps most important is the feeling for *partnership* that this letter reveals. One gets a strong impression of two people united in a mutuality of mission. At the same time, the final decision is definitely "owned" by the one to whom the offer of the new job came, and he's willing to take responsibility for that decision just as the woman in the first letter was able to do. If the other significant people in our lives—those who will be affected by our decisions—have been made part of the process which has brought us to our final decision, then they also will share in its ownership.

One of the longer answers came on tape. This one needs quoting at length, however, since it raises some questions which are pertinent to people who are not living in a partnership relation with another person. The woman who sent the tape is single, in her thirties, and believes that her unique gifts could probably not have been used as effectively in the kinds of ministry she has been called to had she chosen to marry. She says:

> As I've gone through some decision-making processes these last two years and then look back on previous decisions, I can see that there is a pattern. At the moment, however, this pattern is inoperative because a heavy component in the past has been consultation with strong friends, and in my present situation I have no other people who mean that much to me or who care deeply enough about me to participate in my decisions.
>
> When I went to a testing center (required for my present job), they ran me through a battery of tests and one of the areas indicated how one makes decisions. I just laughed at the time because the test showed that I systematically gather as many related facts as I can find and then make a decision based on "gut" reaction to the facts!
>
> I spend a lot of time on major decisions. As time passes, I feel that I'm subconsciously dealing with the matter, although I don't normally make a list of "pros" and "cons."
>
> In the meantime I consult with other people, but basically I'm filtering information through my mind and then when I know what to do, I do it with conviction. It's never a "I wonder if this is the right thing to do" decision, but the step I finally take, I take firmly.
>
> About three or four years ago I was beginning to

feel restless in my job and was realizing that there would be no opportunity for advancement. I was also dating somebody and did not know what either he or I wanted out of that relationship.

All of these factors entered into my consideration of an invitation which might have taken me overseas. I had said no originally, but when a second invitation came from the same source a year later, the relationship with the man was over and did not play a part in my decision. I began the process over again with an entirely different set of "givens."

At that time I began talking to close personal friends about it and especially with people whom I knew were familiar with that area of the world. One of them, an Egyptian well-acquainted with the whole African scene said, "Well, I've been trying not to say anything, but feel that I must." Then he described the political situation there and the upheaval that he felt was surely coming. He said that upheaval was bound to be very tough on Christians in that country, especially if they happened to identify with the "underdogs," which he was sure I would do.

When my parents called a few days later and asked, "What are you going to do about the job?" without even thinking about it, I said very positively, "I'm not going to take it."

My prayers are not, "O God, show me what to do!" but more a sharing of what I'm going through. I'm not saying that "signs" are not given, but it's not a word I normally use. Circumstances are involved in terms of readiness or unreadiness to move or change directions, but I don't have any set way in which I use information. It just all goes into the process and works its way through my head.

After I made the decision mentioned above, I was definitely satisfied and never thought about it again. I was glad it was over and happy I had gone through the process. I was only sorry when I got a letter from the missionary agency saying, "We thought you were all signed, sealed, and delivered, and why aren't you coming?" But I have had no regrets about my decision.

Generally, I feel good about my decision-making process. I remember the time when I was a sophomore in college trying to decide whether or not to change my major from political science to music. Everybody else, including my music teacher and my mother, were trying to influence me to do so. In fact, a letter from my mother at that time, said, "For once in your life make a decision on the basis of emotion!" She knew that emotionally I would rather become a music major, but I didn't. At that time my decision was a life decision, and I felt that I had to make it rationally.

Of course, I have no way of evaluating the results, because I don't know at all what would have happened if I had gone the other way. But I still feel good about my life as a result of that college decision. I sometimes feel bad about some specific small decisions that I make, especially during the past year, but some of that has to do with my sense of isolation in the present job, so that my usual method for decision-making has not been available. That may mean that I need to develop another method at this point or develop the kind of local support-base of friends which will make it operative again in my life.

I think your question about the will of God is a real toughie. It's hard to be so presumptuous as to say that what I'm doing is God's will for me and I *know* that. Yet, I really do feel that's true, and since I can see a very direct linkage in the decisions that have brought me to this point, I see a lot of other decisions as a reflection of God's will for me.

I guess if I couldn't hang on to the conviction that this is God's will for me at this time, I wouldn't be here for as long as I have been, because it's been tough.

Now for the question of marriage. I would probably not have my present job if I had married when most women do. I'm not sure I want to say that it's God's will for me not to be married, yet if I feel that it is God's will for me to be where I am now, and that my being married would not have allowed that to happen, then that *is* what I'm saying.

Almost all those who replied to our questionnaire expressed satisfaction with larger decisions, but several were not always pleased with the smaller, day-by-day decisions. The difference may lie in the amount of time we give to making those life-changing decisions, whereas in the little decisions we act more according to how we feel at the moment.

Some of the factors common to most of the responses we received were these:

1. *Communicating with God through the many forms of prayer.* For many prayer was part of the unconscious processing of data, sort of a substratum of reference

against which all information was evaluated. For others, enlightenment was sought through consciously praying in tongues with the spirit free to receive impressions or messages from the Holy Spirit. In one case a university professor said that she spent half an hour every morning in conversation with God around the question, "What guidance do you have for me today?"

2. *Discussing the matter with* TRUSTED *family members and other friends.* None of the respondents sought indiscriminate advice from strangers or professional advice-givers. Some went to people whom they felt had special gifts of discernment or the ability to see issues clearly. The final decision usually reflected the help of others, but was not necessarily determined by their points of view.

3. *Strong "feelings" played a part, often fortified by hunches, inner convictions, and direct answers to prayer.* No matter how convincing the rational approach, people tended to make the decision on the basis of their feelings. If they did not, they seemed to feel some regret later. "Signs" seemed to be those circumstances or happenings which corroborated feelings.

We have come to believe that it's important not to waste time wondering if the decision you've made is the right one. No one is right all the time, and if you find your choice has been a poor one, then search for and try alternatives. Usually the sharpest period of doubt follows the public announcement of a decision, but then one is caught up in implementing the decision.

4. *Many came to final decisions which were much different from the one they expected to arrive at when they began thinking about it.* While they cannot always un-

derstand why their thinking changed, they are satisfied that the change represents the better course of action and is a definite evidence of guidance.

MARGE: This fall I had a job offer to join the program staff of our district church office. I responded wholeheartedly to the initial questionnaires and requests for my ideas as to how the position should be carried out. Finally came the invitation to meet the search committee for a personal interview. I was one of three persons selected for interview out of all that had been sent the first inquiry.

I prepared carefully for that interview, both in prayer and in thinking through the job description. I felt confident of my ability to do a good job in the position and went to the interview with a high sense of excitement and no nervousness about the impression I would make. Three weeks later, I was offered the job. But, to my own surprise, I no longer felt that I should consider taking it. One question, asked by one of the interviewers, had triggered some thoughts which led me to that conclusion. The question was, "What opportunities for ministry would you have *with* the job that you don't have *now?*"

When I thought my decision through in the context of that question, the answer came out another way. It said that my present life gives me more opportunities for ministry than I would have in a staff position. That doesn't downgrade the position, it just says that for me, at this point in my life, I have some opportunities for ministry both inside and outside the church structures which would not be possible in that job.

I also have to feel that the person who did get the job was the one the Lord wanted in it in the first place, but for some reason I had to go through the process of affirming my own lifestyle now. As a result I have been happy with my decision.

REFLECTION EXERCISE

1. What would *your* answers to the questionnaire at the beginning of this chapter look like?

2. Have you ever experienced some foreknowledge of opportunities that would later come to you, like the woman in the first case study?

3. Does the question, "What opportunities for ministry would you have with the job that you don't have now?" help you make a decision in your own life?

4. What issues does it help to clarify?

8.

How Do I Get It All Together and Keep Going?

MARGE: Looking back on the pages we've written, I think we might have called the chapters something like "running scared," "running wild," "running loose," and then maybe "running free," and now "running home"!

ERLING: To get moving and keep moving now, I have a constant need to zero in on areas where I know energy is available wherever I find it—in the Word, from people, through prayer. I want to keep on taking assignments that are challenging and demanding, but the price that I know I have to pay cuts me short of total dedication because of my own human limitations.

MARGE: Our dreams often seem mismatched with our ability to perform. This happened when we began dreaming about writing this book because we were caught up in our concern for the people who came to us with questions about knowing God's will for their own lives. At that time we were also intrigued because of the situation in our own life and the question we'd been asking, "What are we going to do with the rest of our life?" Now I'm wondering if our writings have matched our dream.

ERLING: I heard a seminary professor speak recently about some work he's doing with his brother who is a psycho-historian, something I had not heard of before. They have been analyzing autobiographies of famous people looking for a common denominator, a basic line that might run through all of these history-making lives.

They've discovered that each one was captivated by one dream above all others. Like St. Paul, they seemed to live out his phrase, "but one thing I do . . ." (Phil. 3:13). So that seems to bear out our insistence on the need to claim your own dream. The people they studied seemed almost to punish themselves in their dedication to their cause. Apparently that's the price you have to pay. Jesus put it neatly when he said that all the commandments can be summed up in the single command to love the Lord with all your soul, mind, strength, and spirit—the totality of your person—and your neighbor as yourself (Matt. 22:36-40).

MARGE: One of the things I resent about writing and yet find absolutely essential is that I must become very anti-social. I can't afford to take time even to talk to people because of my need to be completely absorbed in what I'm writing.

This was especially true when I was writing plays and films. I became the prisoner of the characters in my dramas. They demanded my attention, almost as if they were jealous of the real people in my life. I lived with them and experienced what they experienced and didn't have time for anyone else. Without that kind of single-mindedness that you've been talking about I doubt if any kind of creative work can be done.

ERLING: I met Irving Stone shortly after he had written his book about Michelangelo. He was caught up by his hero and by Michelangelo's compelling need to give form and substance to his visions. In that cause the artist could climb a scaffolding up to the ceiling in the Sistine Chapel at the break of day and lie on his back painting until dark. He forgot about eating; his enemies plotted his death below him; he had opposition from the hierarchy of church and state; but he was so captivated by his dream that it controlled him. Paint could fall in his eyes to the point of blinding him, but still the grand passion drove him on.

As for myself, when I am able to give myself wholeheartedly to my dream, whatever that may be—I move forward in bursts of abundant energy. I'm also aware that at other times nothing flows, and I experience a blockage of all energy.

MARGE: When we talk about "my" Marie Curie and "your" Michelangelo, it all sounds so easy. All I have to do is focus on my dream and—presto!—I can move forward with dedication to accomplish it. Unfortunately, it doesn't seem to work that way very often. Where it's all tested in my life is in the answer to this question, "I wonder if Marie Curie and Michelangelo ever had the same battle that I have with tired flesh? Did Marie ever wake up in her unheated garret, put one foot on the cold floor, pull it back quickly and decide to 'sleep in' that morning?" I find it so easy to do this, and even when I do get up and realize that it's time to start writing, I can find a dozen other things to do first. I wonder if Michelangelo had those same kinds of "little battles" with the flesh, or were his flesh and Marie Curie's flesh made of a different substance than mine? Did they really not need food or sleep? Or does history just ignore such ordinary needs? What I'm looking for is hope for little people like me who are not geniuses. What are the keys for living the common life of dedication?

ERLING: My hope is to be not a powerhouse but just a bulb at one end of a power line, illuminated and illuminating. I want to duplicate in my experience the reality of Jesus' experience when he knew that the Spirit of the Lord was upon him and he went out to do his Father's assignments. The answer lies in ways of rediscovering this energy—the power of the Spirit—during the times when the vision, the dream, the desire, the willingness are all there, but nothing seems to be happening. We get caught in an energy crisis of one kind or another.

We've tried classifying some of the energy crises that stall our spirits.

One of those could be labeled *untapped energy*. This can come from that poor self-image that often afflicts us. We just don't think we have anything going for us. The energy is there, but we don't believe it, so it's never tapped. No matter how much others try to convince us that we've got what it takes to produce, we'll deny it vigorously. We continue to compare ourselves with others and always rate ourselves as a "zero."

A second kind of energy crisis is *inadequate energy*, a condition in which we admit that we do have some energy, but it's not really enough to do anything. From this comes that sense of powerlessness that finds expression in the attitude, "What can one person do? My vote doesn't really count. Only the big shots really have anything to say about what happens." I admit that I have *some* power, but I discount it by saying that it really doesn't amount to much; it's not adequate to accomplish anything very important.

Then there's the feeling of *restricted energy*. "I could do it if I had the opportunity. But opportunity never knocks on my door." Minority persons express this; women chafe under laws that restrict their energies; persons with physical handicaps often have brilliant minds, but the energy required to move through the simple daily routines depletes the amount of energy left for creativity. Many socioeconomic groups just don't have the energy for education and extensive training, because the energy required to survive greatly depletes what's needed for intellectual, technological, and artistic pursuits.

One could be suffering from *undernourished energy*, which means that the sources are known and available, but we're too lazy or poorly motivated to tap them—like taking time for peripheral activities rather than zeroing in on the more productive ones.

Or maybe that's really *wasted energy* which comes from having such poorly defined goals that we don't know what we want or where we're going, so we just run around in circles. You can't get organized because you don't know what it is you want to organize toward.

So many of our energy crises are ways of saying that we really don't want to be captured by a dream—that God's call to servanthood is not worth the price we're asked to pay in terms of total dedication! We lapse into biding time, listening to the ticking of the clock, and even searching for ways to "kill time." Instead of the channel of God's grace it's meant to be, time squeezes into a meaningless vacuum of inactivity, and we sit around waiting for another "vision" or another "zapping" by the Spirit of God.

We need to share one way in which we ministered to one another during the writing of this book. There came the usual and predictable dry season; we were completely bogged down, wasting time, putting it off.

We really believe that we are "born again" each day in a daily dying to self and rising to God through the Holy Spirit. In practice, it works this way for us. Let's agree that all of the "energy crises" we've listed above reflect sin. If I don't love myself, that's sin. If I'm deploying my God-given energy in self-pity, worry, feelings of dependency and inadequacy, that's sin. If I don't know why I'm in the world; if I have no vision of what my life is all about; if I don't know where I'm headed; that's sin. The Bible tells us that God has called us with a "holy" calling to servanthood. If I don't believe that, that's sin. If I'm born again into newness of life in Christ, then "all things are possible" the Word tells me. When I'm denying this by saying, "I can't do this" or "I can't do that," that's sin. Since God calls us to ministry, it's his promise that I will get all that I need to perform that ministry. If I don't believe that, that's sin.

When we realize that this kind of "sinful" thinking is miring us in the quicksands of unbelief, the answer is to confess and be forgiven. For us it's helpful to do that in each other's presence, especially where we are involved in a partnership ministry such as this book. Anything that keeps us from fulfilling that ministry we consider a "sickness" of the spirit. So we follow the principle given in James 5:16, "Confess your faults to one another, that you may be healed." You might find this a little difficult at first, because we are spiritually inhibited beings. We who talk so freely about the most intimate matters—even observing them discussed on television in the most obvious ways—are nevertheless embarrassed about the intimate things of our spirits.

MARGE: This is what we did. I came to Erling and said, "I feel helpless, without power. That feeling is choking whatever creativity I may have. Will you listen to my confession?"

As we said, it isn't easy, especially with your own husband or wife—maybe less easy because of being that close. Yet, the whole concept of "partnership in the gospel" becomes more meaningful when that partnership is exercised in that most basic of Christian behaviors, confession and forgiveness of sins.

At first I usually find myself being very general as even our liturgies tend to be when we unite in confessing that "I am by nature sinful and unclean," but as we become more specific, we become more honest in confession. So I was able to admit, "Right now, I am procrastinating. I'm indulging my own laziness because I'd rather lie down and take a nap or read a magazine instead of forcing myself to sit at the typewriter. I'd rather go out and work in the garden because I'm really not very caught up in the ministry of writing. I feel rebellious against the whole idea of ministry and having to work at it!"

ERLING: When Marge had finished with her honest outpouring, I was enabled to confess my own joylessness. She asked, "Can you identify what lies behind your joylessness?" I had to confess that it feeds on the fact that I am guilty of holding back some of the expression of thankfulness for the healing of my paralysis. I want *more* healing; I focus on what I *don't* have rather than giving praise for the fact that I can walk and work. So I feel sorry for myself, complaining about my remaining physical disabilities and using them as an excuse to dump most of the work of writing on Marge. (It wasn't easy for me to admit that directly to her, although it had bothered me a good deal in private.) In confession, I began to see how much that kind of thinking limits me from being able to do what I want to do. My energies don't flow as they ought, but are wasted in the futility of self-pity.

As we continued to confess to one another, we experienced the dying to self that the Bible expresses as God's means of daily renewal. The more uninhibited and specific we became in revealing what was really behind those "bogged down feelings," the more we began to see the whole thing as a matter of priorities. We tend to put so many things before our commitment to ministry; we put the house first, the things we *like* to do first, our aches and pains first, our feelings first. Our flow of energy was turned off right at the First Commandment, "You shall have no other gods before me," or in New Testament words, "But seek first his kingdom and his righteousness, and all these things shall be yours as well" (Matt. 6:33).

We had made a commitment to the Lord to write this book as part of our ministry, and we were not putting that first. In our confession we realized that was the reason our energies were bottled up. Michelangelo's primary commitment was not to the people who hired him. Long before that he had committed his talent to God, and from the Lord he had received his vision of that amazing painting, and from the Lord he was receiving the strength to complete it. Marie Curie's passionate dedication to the welfare of humanity motivated her to give away all that she had learned about radium without any thought of gain for herself. In fact, her intense overexposure to radiation eventually caused her death. Nothing can dam up energy that stays focused on the dream as priority!

MARGE: When we had made confession to one another, then we pronounced on each other God's absolution, the forgiveness of sins. I was able to say to Erling, "Because of the grace of God given to me in Jesus Christ, I can share with you the assurance that your sins are forgiven. Be renewed in your energies and work in peace."

ERLING: I was able to say the same to Marge, telling her that God had forgiven her and that he had set her apart in power for the writing task. Then we sensed that energy began to flow. Our minds were opened as they had not been before in that amazing miracle of God's infinite source of grace which is always released in the act of confession and forgiveness.

MARGE: After our informal "liturgy," I felt imbued with new life, and a strength of the Spirit filled my entire body. Everything that had previously been hindering me from knowing what we wanted to communicate through this book was gone. The end of our writing might not be a classic, but it would at least be an expression of all that God's Spirit could say through us at this time.

Yet when I had tried on my own initiative to be creative and bright, I had sensed a continual "missing of the mark" which is a direct translation of the Greek word for "sin."

If at this point in your life you feel bogged down, stalled, unable to move or to feel any motivation to get on with the living of your life; if you don't have a sense of direction or care about finding a sense of direction; then maybe you need to confess to the Lord that sin of apathy and lack of commitment to ministry. Why not stop reading for a while and experience this act of worship, "Lord, I need to make confession to you right now that there are hindrances in me to the flow of your power and energy. The fun has gone out of my commitment, and duty, instead of love, is running my life. Lord, I confess. . . ." If you have a "partner" at hand, make your confession to that person and listen to the words of forgiveness as they apply to you. Alone, or with another, accept your cleansing.

On the day we conducted our private confessional service, we were able to complete three chapters of our book! We spent the evening in praise, and in that continuing worship discovered again the joy in the Spirit who empowers all of our ministries for our Lord.

Your confession of need is an act of faith which opens you up to God's grace. In the acceptance of that grace you are set free, wherever you are now, from the binding and haunting circumstances of your past, the limitations of your body, your own feelings of inadequacy and nervousness, free to mesh your dreams with God's dream for you.

Are you beginning to see your ministry? Is the path marked out for fulfilling your servanthood becoming clearer? Do you see the choices, big and little, that you must make to walk that path? Will you appropriate the strength and enlightenment you need from God's Spirit?

As you take your next step on that path, perhaps with some hesitation, you will experience that the answer to the question, "Who's running your life?" is without a doubt, *"I am, with the help of God!"*

Bethlehem Lutheran Church
Two Harbors, Minn.

Bethlehem Lutheran Church
Two Harbors, Minn.